The Elements of Learning

· · · · · · · · · · · · ·

The Elements of Learning

James M. Banner, Jr.

Harold C. Cannon

Yale University Press ■ New Haven and London

Published with assistance from the Kingsley Trust Association
Publication Fund established by the Scroll and Key Society
of Yale College.

Designed by Sonia Scanlon
Set in Syntax with Tekton display type by Tseng Information Systems,
Durham, N.C.
Printed in the United States of America by Vail-Ballou Press,
Binghamton, New York.

Library of Congress Cataloging-in-Publication Data
Banner, James M., 1935–
The elements of learning / James M. Banner, Jr.,
and Harold C. Cannon.
    p.   cm.
ISBN 0-300-07836-6 (alk. paper)
1. Learning. 2. Study skills. 3. Learning, Psychology of.
4. College student orientation. I. Cannon, Harold C., 1930–
II. Title.
LB1060.B36 1999
378.1'70281—dc21   98-50161

A catalogue record for this book is available from the British Library.

10 9 8 7 6 5 4 3 2 1

Contents . . . .

Preface ....

The first book we wrote together, *The Elements of Teaching*, was about the human qualities of instruction—the qualities involved in being a teacher. This book is about the human qualities of learning—the qualities involved in being a student.

We've written it for students of all ages who are studying any subject and seeking knowledge in any situation at any level of schooling. Yet we also have written it with a particular group of students more centrally in mind—those who are in the last two years of high school and the first two years of college. These are the years when people come to maturity as students and can make the best use of their opportunities to learn. Paradoxically, they're also years of confusion about almost everything, a time when studying may seem the most unpleasant and irrelevant activity in which to be involved, even though learning is the best way to get a bearing on life.

We also have in mind those students who return to the classroom later in their lives. Because they often find themselves out of practice after having spent years away from formal schooling, they may find reminders of the challenges and satisfactions of learning useful as they embark on academic work again.

In addition, we want to help those who may no longer be students themselves (at least in a formal sense) but who are deeply involved in students' lives and concerned about their welfare. We hope that such people—schoolteachers, college professors, and students' parents above all—will find the book appropriate to their needs and worthy of their attention. For everyone was once a student, and recalling what we thought and felt in our school days—an exercise we've put ourselves through while writing the book—ought to bring to mind the personal qualities that students need if they're to gain the knowledge they must have. Students benefit enormously when people who understand their circumstances, fears, and confusions offer compassionate and sensible encouragement and support. They may also find it easier to accept the advice of strangers, like the authors of this book, than the wisdom of their teachers and parents.

In preparing the book, we have been greatly assisted by Gideon B. Banner, Olivia P. Banner, Christine R. Bannerman, Betty M. Cannon, Julia Clark-Spohn, Barbara C. Follansbee, Dennis Gray, Sally Hermsdorfer, Alison Hilton, Phyllis Hirschkop, Gwin J. Kolb, Bryce V. Lambert, Terrence Reynolds, Eileen Sheehy, and Joseph P. Viteritti, each of whom, perennial students all, read and evaluated a draft of the manuscript. All helped us improve and reflect more deeply on what we had written. From our colleagues at Yale University Press, both in New Haven and in London, we have received constant support, encouragement, and professional assistance for this book and its predecessor. In particular, we are grateful to Dan Heaton for his keen editorial skills and to Charles Grench for his sage counsel and thoughtful guidance. We absolve all of responsibility for any errors the work may contain or any arguments with which they may disagree.

How to Read This Book

You don't have to read this book from front to back. Nor, to gain its benefits, do you have to read all of it. We've organized the book to make it easy to use as best suits your own purposes and to help you dip into it without getting lost. We know that you'll be searching for help about matters that challenge or trouble you the most, and we think that's a good approach.

The chapters of Part I, The Elements of Learning, outline the qualities you need as a student—industry, enthusiasm, pleasure, curiosity, aspiration, imagination, self-discipline, civility, cooperation, honesty, and initiative. Each chapter contains some general reflections, some suggestions about how to think about the nature and development of the quality that is the subject of the chapter, and an illustrative sketch of a student (fictional in every case, but drawn from our experiences) who either embodies that quality or falls short of embodying it.

Part II, The Circumstances of Learning, comprises chapters meant to help you understand the environment in which you study and learn. They concern your teachers, the curriculum that gives structure to your education, the ways you can learn, and the transition between school and college.

Throughout, we've interspersed suggestions— "what to do's"—of other ways you can improve the range and depth of your knowledge and increase your power to learn. These, too, can be read in any order that proves useful.

Although the book is focused principally on formal education, we don't mean to suggest that you don't also learn much outside the classroom or that what we have to say here can't help you in the workplace. On the contrary:

we believe that what we've written can be of use to you in many places besides school and college. But in the conviction that the qualities you need to learn when you're studying carry over into the rest of your life, we've devoted most of our attention to what goes on in educational institutions and have drawn most of our illustrations from school and college situations.

Also, we don't mean to suggest that the only way to learn is to study, or that you ought to consider giving up everything else—family life and social and other extra-curricular activities—while you're in school or college. Far from it. Balance is required as much when you're deeply involved in studying as in the rest of your life. Nothing we say should be taken to mean otherwise. Nevertheless, because this book is about studying and learning, that's where we've put our emphasis.

If you're not going to college or if you plan to postpone doing so for a few years, no harm will be done if you don't read Chapter 16, which concerns the challenges of going directly from school to college. Skipping that chapter won't hurt because the rest of the book pertains directly to that other major part of your education—your high school experience.

In short, read and use the book in any way that you think best.

The Elements of Learning
· · · · · · · · · · · · ·

1

. . . .

The Adventure of Learning

If you were the best student you could be, what qualities would you possess?

You may answer that those qualities would include intelligence, mathematical ability, language skills, and practical expertise in studying and taking tests. And if you're studying music, say, or dance, or art, you'll say that you would want also to develop qualities of listening, bodily movement, and perception. Good qualities, certainly, and all helpful. But they alone can't get you far. You also need qualities to ensure that what you're learning will stick in your mind and senses and ripen into genuine understanding. For that to happen, you need the elements of learning—the human qualities that enable you to learn what you need (and choose) to know and achieve.

You've probably not given these elements of learning much thought. Not many people have, even those who devote their lives to teaching you. Yet these elements are critically important to your welfare as a student—and to your entire life. Being a good student may seem no more than a phase without inherent value, but learning can often be its own good. You learn because of a keen appetite for understanding, because of the sheer joy of knowing, and because of the deep satisfaction of possessing knowledge—simply because knowledge exists and because you want to have it.

Moreover, being a good student is a means to ends beyond the obvious. It is one of the principal means by which you learn about life in all its complexity and wonder. Only through knowledge of yourself and the world around you can you form yourself fully. Through studying and learning, you understand who you are, what you want to achieve, and how you can achieve it. The elements of learning are therefore the qualities you need to become the person you want to be.

Equally important, by developing and gaining understanding of the elements of learning, you take responsibility for your own development. You're not born a student, nor do you become one by enrolling in school or college. Being a student is something you have to learn to be, a role you must grow into. The best schools and colleges, the best teachers and professors, the best courses in the world can't achieve anything for you without your active engagement. Only you can turn yourself into a student. Only you can get yourself to learn.

We've written this book to help you understand how to become the best student you can be during the time when you have the privilege of attending school or college. Our book has no magic powers. It won't tell you directly how to get good grades, take tests, or study. It won't assist you in learning to dance, play an instrument, or act on the stage. It won't even advise you about specific courses to take. Those are important considerations, but they're not as important as learning how to undertake your education. We want you to understand the inner qualities, not the methods and skills, on which to base your education. When you've developed these qualities, then you will be more capable of facing the challenges of tests and papers, of laboratory experiments and acting exercises.

We're presuming, of course, that you want to be a good student, and a better one than you are now—or why would you be reading this book at all? Yet you may not know what it takes to be a student in the full meaning of that term, and our guess is that nobody has taken the time to explain it to you, which seems to us unfair. Surely, no one has patrolled the halls of your school or the dormitories of your college repeating, "Think what it means to be a good student!" Yet that's what we want you to think about.

After all, in most other enterprises you're carefully prepared for your experiences. If you find yourself serving on a jury, the trial judge will explain your responsibilities to you before the trial begins—and your responsibilities will be over in a few days. If you're due for an operation, your doctor will explain to you why the procedure is necessary and what you can expect from it—and your convalescence will usually take at most a matter of weeks. But being a full-time student can last for two decades, and it affects your entire life. Being a student is an adventure, for which you have to be prepared if it's to be fully satisfying and beneficial. So shouldn't you find out how to equip yourself to get the most out of it?

Why listen to us? What makes us dependable guides on this journey?

First of all, we love to teach, and we love the subjects we teach—classics for one of us, history for the other. Between us, we've been teaching students from elementary grades through university graduate school and beyond for more than sixty years. Also, we like students and being around them. After all, why would we have spent so many years in your company if we didn't choose to share your struggles and triumphs? We know that the future always belongs to students. We like playing a role in helping others learn about our subjects and about themselves. We know what it takes to study and to learn, and we want to tell you what we know.

We're parents, too, and so we've taught our children. We were also once students like you—and like you, no doubt, sometimes drove our teachers half-crazy with our behavior or with our reluctance to learn what they were trying to teach us. And we have remained students throughout our careers, reading seriously and writing for publication in our fields of expertise. The fact that we've been working with students for so long has helped keep us up-to-date about classroom conditions and problems in schools and colleges.

Yet even with all our experience as students, we didn't encounter many of the difficulties you may face. When we were young, discipline was stronger, the authority of our teachers and professors was less open to challenge, social issues seldom invaded our classrooms, and many of today's serious distractions, such as drugs and crime, were much less intrusive. The absence of such challenges made it easier for us to be students than you probably find it, and it is in part because of changes in schools and colleges that we've written this book.

We also want the book to help you understand the confusions and feelings you experience as you struggle to learn. We remember those feelings all too well—how we wished our teachers would go easy on us, how we wanted to be with our friends rather than our books, how we envied other students who had an easier time learning. We want to help you understand and overcome such natural feelings.

So we've written out of compassion rather than out of an urge to preach. During our careers as teachers, we have known many students in our courses who didn't know why they were there, except that they had to take a certain number of courses to graduate. We have tried to help make their experiences more rewarding and enduring. We've tried to show them that, with all the hard work that is necessary, the discovery of knowledge can also be exciting, liberating, and enriching, and that studying and learning can bring great pleasures. We want to do the same for you.

We prescribe no hard-and-fast rules, which rarely do much good anyway. Instead, we offer you suggestions about how you can become a good student, think of yourself as one, and enjoy yourself as much as you can in the process. And we believe that our suggestions can be helpful to those—your teachers, parents, relatives, and friends—who are assisting you with your education, all those people who want to see you succeed but aren't always sure what advice to give you.

We admit that there's much to dislike about being a student. You're controlled and directed by adults who are always evaluating you, seeking proof of your progress. Your grades cause you anguish, anxiety, and sometimes embarrassment. You probably dislike some of your required courses and being herded from room to room throughout the day at the sound of bells. Perhaps worst of all are the people who always tell you what's best for you without explaining why.

We know that learning is hard, very hard. It requires arduous work, much of it sheer drudgery. Often you'd rather be doing something else that yields quick and easy pleasures rather than working for something, like understanding, that may be beyond the range of your vision. When we were students, we often felt as if we'd been sentenced to life at hard labor with no chance for parole.

Yet for all its difficulties, learning is a privilege in a world that so often ignores the welfare of its young people. That's why you may think that your education is a right, something owed to you, rather than a privilege, an opportunity whose benefits you have to earn. It's a privilege in the sense that you can't rely upon your school or college to undertake something in your behalf unless you make an effort to meet your responsibilities at the same time. The reciprocity, the dynamic interrelationship between you and the other members of the institution at which you're studying, promotes your education. We also say that education is a privilege because it's offered to you when your chief obligation should be to yourself and to your intellectual growth. Not until much later in life are you likely to have the relative liberty you now enjoy as a student, even in the midst of other responsibilities, to attend to yourself and to your own best interests. The trick is to know how to make the most of this unique time in your life.

The adventure of learning, like all adventures, is full of surprises, excitement, and enjoyment. It's not all unrelieved hard work. It doesn't require you to give up laughter or to stay at your desk forever or to practice the piano all day long. In fact, it's something you can enjoy, as long as you're prepared for it—as long as you develop certain human qualities.

These qualities—industry, enthusiasm, pleasure, curiosity, aspiration, imagination, self-discipline, civility, cooperation, honesty, and initiative—are good not just for high school or college. They're good for life and for most of life's situations. Yet no one is born with all these qualities. Nor do they develop by themselves. You must acquire them and then strengthen and maintain them by continual effort. Intelligence may be a genetic gift, but applying intelligence effectively requires the qualities we stress in this book. In return, what you gain through study helps these very qualities mature.

Thus when you make the most of your opportunities as a student, you draw less on techniques or skills you've learned than on the internal capacities you already possess and ought to perfect. You don't *get* an education; you *make* one out of your inner resources. You summon from within yourself the qualities that make your education productive. What you achieve as a student can't be separated from who you are.

Being a student is a state of mind, a way of looking at what you're doing. Being a student means that you bring your qualities as a person to bear upon studying and learning. Being a student involves taking responsibility for your education. When you learn to do so, you become not only a good student but someone who is free to follow learning wherever it may lead.

Part One

· ·

The Elements of Learning

Industry

By definition, real students work hard. If you don't work hard, you're not a real student; you're either a genius or a slacker. For most of us—people who have to work to achieve what we want and can't rely on genius to achieve it—success in studying, as in everything else, requires hard, sometimes extremely hard, work. The good news, however, is that hard work brings great rewards.

It's the same in every field of endeavor. Even the most talented people must struggle to master the rudiments of their art, perfect their skills, and learn what they need to know. Piano and violin prodigies and math geniuses, for instance—people whose talents are so extraordinary that we term their abilities "gifts," as if their skills are given to them and not worked for—even these students must struggle to master their instruments or complete their mathematical breakthroughs by unremitting, exhausting application, which sometimes bores them and often wears them out.

Study is therefore the opposite of indulgence and indolence. It calls for repeated application, concentration, focused thought, and often solitude—all challenging demands. Although study can bring you great pleasure and rewards, actual study is often tedious. Its satisfactions come in its results, rarely in the activity of studying itself. Its benefits are often postponed far into the

Working on Your Weaknesses

It helps to think of studying as an athlete thinks of training or as an instrumentalist thinks of practicing. In demanding enterprises like these, you can't perform to the peak of your ability without concentrating your attention where it's needed—say, on your swing, so that you can hit the baseball harder, or on finger exercises, so that you can play scales and arpeggios on the piano faster and more accurately.

It should be the same with studying and learning. Once you have identified your weaknesses, you should work hard at eliminating or compensating for them.

Let your strengths carry you. If you're a tennis player, you shouldn't work to perfect your already strong serve until you get your weak backhand in shape. Similarly, as a student, you shouldn't focus on improving your strong skills in math until you improve your weak writing ability. In both cases, you're better off relying on what you do well while you concentrate on improving what you do less well. That way, you raise the overall level of your abilities and become a stronger student in every way, better able to respond to challenges and reach what you set out to achieve.

But don't rest on your laurels. Once you find it relatively easy to do what once was difficult, give yourself a new, tougher challenge. Are you beginning to get A's in courses where you once got C's? Then turn to those subjects in which you still get C's and work to bring your grades up

there. Common sense, you'll say. Yes indeed, but it's easy to
kid yourself into thinking that in reaching one goal, you've
done about all that you can do. That's never the case. Life's
never that easy.

Be honest with yourself. Address your shortcomings candidly and without fear. Remind yourself that what
you know least you need most. Tell yourself that what you
have the most trouble doing demands your attention and
improvement. There's nothing like the satisfaction of knowing that you've done better than you could before. But you
can't experience that satisfaction if you try to fool yourself.

indiscernible future. Studying and learning are therefore the opposite
of all the material trophies that our commercial culture extols.

We know that emphasizing the importance of industry is
not an enticing way to start an early chapter in a book about what it
means to be a student, especially when we want you to read on because we believe that what we have to say is important to your welfare. Perhaps we should have waited until the end to throw a bucket
of ice water over you, rather than doing so at the beginning. But
whether you like to hear it or not, diligence and persistence are required if you're going to be a good student. Hard work when you're
in school and college is like a wise investment: its capital grows, its
interest compounds, and its dividends pile up.

There are two principal benefits of hard work. The first is
knowledge—although often you can't foresee its value, for knowledge has a way of teasing you with the unpredictability of its meaning and use. The second benefit of hard work is made up of the
products of knowledge. They include the inventions that help give
our world some comfort, health, and security, as well as an under-

standing of how the conditions under which we live have come to exist. Automobiles, elevators, and computers were not created by lazy, inactive minds, nor were the plays of Shakespeare, the paintings of Rembrandt, or the theories of Einstein achieved in couch-bound stupors. In fact, we might say of learning what the great inventor Thomas Edison once said of genius—it's 1 percent inspiration, 99 percent perspiration. Edison wanted to remind us that the achievements of genius, which we all enjoy and benefit from, result from unceasing efforts of mind and will. And so it is with all learning: industry is demanded, laziness will not serve. Little of value comes easily. Put another way, if you think studying is costly, try ignorance.

Only by study—only by such demanding acts as purposeful reading, memorization, research, and writing—can you expose yourself fully to the infinite dimensions of life. You can learn much by reading newspapers or watching television. But what you're getting there is information, which is not the same as knowledge. You go to school and college to learn how to transform information into knowledge and understanding, not just to memorize facts or to "pick up" bits and pieces of what's known.

Once you have enough knowledge to glimpse new worlds of understanding and emotional and spiritual satisfaction that you never before imagined or experienced, you can commit yourself to even more demanding work and do better than you've ever thought possible. And you can do so without turning against your teachers, as the students of John Scotus Erigena, a philosopher in the court of the Holy Roman Empire, turned on him many centuries ago. John's students stabbed him to death with their pens because he tried to force them to think.

That story touches every student (and cautions every teacher). By and large, none of us, young or old, student or not, likes to work hard. Most of us tend to resent any pressures, whether from parents or teachers, to grapple with our natural laziness and inertia. And so, instead of fighting ourselves, we fight others. That kind of

resistance may work for a while. We may get away with murder—
even literally, as John's students did. But in the long run, the student
who doesn't take advantage of the opportunity to study loses out.
True, industry doesn't determine everything. Just as there
are people whose native gifts lift them high in accomplishment without back-breaking labor, so there are others who "succeed"—by
becoming wealthy or by rising high in their chosen occupations—
without having been industrious or self-disciplined in school and
college. Perhaps they're especially talented, but more likely they're
lucky. Whatever the case, often they admit to having missed out on
one benefit that those who studied hard have gained: knowledge of
a wide range of subjects and deeper understanding of most. They're
the ones often heard to remark that they wish they had worked
harder in school and college. They have learned late in life, often too
late to do them much good, what they wished they'd learned earlier
—that the hard work of study can pay the greatest dividend life has
to offer: understanding of life itself. That—not celebrity or wealth—
is why you must try so hard to learn.

We know that gifts, abilities, and skills are not evenly dis-
tributed. What comes easily to one person is a high hurdle to another.
One subject bores you silly, another is a never-ending source of wonder and delight. Similarly, just as different subjects attract different
people, so studying diligently means something different to different
people; and the ability to study hard often depends on a student's
circumstances and temperament and even the schools and colleges
he or she attends.

Take, for instance, a serious student who attends a school
that focuses on its athletic teams. The student likes sports and plays
on the varsity basketball team. But others make fun of her because
she always wants to go to the library to study, to excel in class, and
to get into a good college. So she has to overcome odds that a student at a school with a different atmosphere doesn't have to face—a
school, for example, with a principal who keeps sports in perspective,

who sees that nothing in the school takes precedence over academic work and achievement, and who makes sure that the names of the school's Merit Scholar finalists are posted on the school's outdoor notice board along with the football team's conference championship. In such a school, where the main emphasis is on aspiration and respect for knowledge, this student would have an easier time of it, and her work would be better respected and rewarded. As it is, though, she's at a serious disadvantage; her school is not helping her be the student she wants to be.

Our parents used to tell us that hard work never killed anyone, but we weren't convinced. At the least, we were certain that hard work had injured and incapacitated a great many victims. It often kept us from being with our friends, for example, or doing something else we preferred. But we eventually learned that while nobody relishes back-breaking (or mind-breaking) labor under any circumstances, most people welcome it if it's undertaken with some clearly defined and beneficial purpose in mind.

Students who work hard will probably enjoy some measure of success, of course, and those who don't will generally do less well. There are exceptions to this rule, but the dullards and sloths who succeed and the geniuses who fail are so rare as to confirm the general rule. If you aspire to the heights of knowledge and achievement, it's probably a good idea to climb the ladder step by step rather than sit around waiting to sprout a pair of wings.

■

The motivations for studying hard, just like those for practicing sports hard, vary greatly. Some students do so out of pride, some in pursuit of high grades. Others fall under the influence of a hypnotic teacher or become intrigued with the challenge and complexity of a subject itself. No matter what the case, you need at least one good reason to study. When you furnish your own motivation to study, instead of having it imposed on you, you're most ready to learn. If you can hold fast to that motivation as your purpose and reason for working hard, then it's likely to keep you on the job much more effectively than any teacher's reprimand or parent's warning.

It's not difficult, however, to think that you're studying hard when you're not—or at least to think that you're working as hard as you can when you could be doing much more. For learning takes special kinds of hard work, the kinds that engage the mind and are therefore particularly difficult to sustain—more difficult, for instance, than repeated efforts to shoot a ball into an iron hoop or to leap over a bar that's higher than your head. What do we mean?

✔ *Learning requires you to make an unending effort to keep your mind on what you're studying.* The human mind seems to wander off at the first chance and refuses to stay tuned to anything for more than a few minutes without great acts of will. You suddenly find yourself daydreaming or watching a classmate clown around instead of listening to your teacher. Or you can't keep your attention on a lesson as long as you'd like because of some difficulty with your vision. For all sorts of reasons, many of us have to summon almost superhuman strength to attach our minds to their current tasks. Yet that's one of the greatest challenges you face as a student—to keep your mind close to you and to what you're being asked to learn, especially when your mind would rather wander a million miles away. Your teachers know that, and they're experienced enough to catch your glazed expression when you're off in some other galaxy and to understand the difficulty you have in staying focused on your lessons. But don't expect them to be responsible for calling you to attention. You've got to make that effort yourself.

✔ *Your hardest job is to study and learn alone.* By the time you reach high school, you're on your own for much of your learning. In college, you spend even less of your time learning in classroom situations. Most of your collegiate study takes place in the library, laboratory, or elsewhere, your only company being the books you're learning from. Study takes place in private, and ideas don't cross the space between a page and your brain of their own accord. You have to work at it yourself, where there's no one to keep after

Why Teachers Work You So Hard

Good teachers challenge you every minute you're in their presence, and really good teachers continue to challenge you even when they're not around. Having been students themselves, they know that you'd probably prefer to be doing something else than studying and learning, and so they try to overcome your preferences with their enthusiastic and remorseless encouragement. This may distress you, and you may wonder why they have to make you work so hard. But if they didn't do so, they wouldn't be doing their jobs.

If we're right in presuming that you wish to learn, would you prefer that your teachers let you drift, gave you no assignments, told nothing but stories in class, and gave you what, in earlier days, was known as a "gentleman's C"? Bad students want easy teachers. Good students hope for ones who push them and expect the most that they can give.

You've surely noticed that your best teachers keep moving the goal line of achievement just beyond your reach, just beyond the line at which you scored your previous academic touchdown. They know your potential, and they're always pushing you—pulling you, really—to go that extra yard or two beyond anything you've ever thought possible, in an ever-intensifying competition against yourself.

Yet the pleasure they get from pushing you so hard is not sadistic; it's altruistic. They push you hard for your

sake, not theirs. Your progress in learning is their chief satisfaction, and it is therefore no charity to go easy on you. Your
teachers make learning hard for you because they must—
because that's the only way good teachers can teach.

If you watch them carefully, you'll see how your
teachers are luring you to work hard through well-tried
tricks of their trade. They try, for example, to arouse your
curiosity about something so that, fascinated by the subject, you'll extend yourself to find out more about it on your
own. They require you to rewrite a paper rather than giving
it a low mark because they know better than you do that
you can improve your writing only if you put in more work.

Such incentives can work wonders for you. But
your teachers' tricks can go only so far. Their real purpose is
to instill in you a lifelong habit of pushing yourself because
of the expectations they've set for you, which then become
your own.

you but yourself, no one else to confirm whether or not you're succeeding to learn.

✔ *Industry is most evident and beneficial when you go
beyond what you're required to study and learn.* When you go further than required, you are choosing to learn what you want to learn,
and you're forming your mind to fit your interests. Most assignments
represent the minimum your instructors believe you must know. And
who can be satisfied with that? When you are prepared to enlarge
your knowledge of any subject on your own by going into it in greater
depth than an assignment demands, by searching for ways to understand it in ways you're comfortable with, or by following your own
curiosity, then that assignment should kindle as much puzzlement in
you as understanding. Rather than cultivating a satisfied (and self-

deluding) sense that you know all there is to know about the business, you'll find yourself wanting to get to the root of it.

✔   *The effort of studying and learning requires organization.* Every effort to learn takes time, and going beyond what's assigned requires you to commit even more time to study. That may appear too much to ask. After all, if you're in high school, you're already putting in at least thirty hours of classwork per week, and then you may have a part-time job after school. The number of "contact hours" drops off in college, possibly to fifteen hours or less per week, but assignments are longer and more demanding than those in high school, and you may still have to work to help pay for your education. As a student you probably can't get the job done in forty hours, the conventional measure of the adult workweek. So there's no getting around the fact that studying and learning require a planned and scheduled commitment of time if you're to be the best student you can be.

It's always easier to work hard when someone's standing over you, encouraging you, and keeping you up to the mark. The trouble with being a student is that you don't have such mentors most of the time. You have to carry out much of your best work unsupervised and alone—and that can make you feel lonely. But it also means that you have the freedom to take charge of your own education, with all the exhilaration that such responsibility entails, if only you'll seize it.

So while you are free to goof off and neglect your studies, you're also free to buckle down and get some real work done. We'd vote for that kind of independence any time, if only because we believe that everyone has the right to self-determination. But the challenge of that measure of freedom is that you must consider your own best interests and create your own discipline—that is, self-discipline, always preferable to the imposed kind.

Richard Lazinski's potential was universally recognized, but he never applied himself to achieving it. His friends found his conversation dazzling because he remembered everything he had ever read. He could talk intelligibly about black holes and explain the political geography of the Balkans as readily as he could evaluate the anticrime efforts of urban police forces. Not surprisingly, he got straight A's every semester. At least he did until he met up with Professor McCormick of the English department.

Susan McCormick was considered one of the best teachers on the faculty: an exciting lecturer, accessible to students, understanding, and fair. She sensed when a student was going through emotional difficulties, when a student hadn't slept the night before, or when a student was faking completion of an assignment. And she had a reputation for expecting much of her students, evaluating each one's work impartially and taking into account each one's way of learning.

Richard eagerly anticipated learning Shakespeare from Professor McCormick. When the course began, he attended her lectures and discussions regularly. At midterm he handed in what he thought was a characteristically strong paper on Shakespeare's sonnets. Professor McCormick handed it back to him with a C.

"A C?" he stormed to his friends. "I've never gotten a C in my life!" He was no more modest in his protests to Professor McCormick. "How could you give me a C?" he asked her. "I read Shakespeare. I gave you the twenty pages you wanted. So why'd you give me a C?" "Because that's what it's worth," Professor McCormick calmly explained to him. "Clearly you had the sonnets open in front of you when you wrote the paper. You quote each one accurately. But there's not a fresh idea in the paper; everything there had already been said in class. There's no evidence that you've given a moment of your own thought to what you've read. Do the poems say what others think they say? Do you find nothing in Shakespeare that stimulates your own thinking? Do you take no issue with others who have read him?"

Professor McCormick explained to Richard that the grade was an estimation not of his mind or character but only of the paper he'd submitted. And true to her reputation, she held out an irresistible offer to him. "Do you want me to consider this a first draft so that you can do the paper over? If you do better, your new grade will replace the C." Richard accepted the offer and the challenge gratefully.

When he returned with a revised paper, he was sheepish and apologetic. "I think you're right about that first paper," he told Professor McCormick. "I should have been angry at myself, not you. This one's better." She agreed—and gave it an A-minus. "What have your other professors been giving you for papers like that first one?" she asked him when he returned to pick up his revised paper. "A's," he reported. Unsurprised, she remarked: "Then their standards are different from mine, and in my classroom, my standards are the only ones that count. You've shown that you can do A-level work, but not by coasting."

But, Richard wondered, why not coast? I'm bright by nature. I can get mostly A's—unless I run into someone tough like McCormick. So why work harder when I can't get any higher grades anyway? No sweat, more fun, he concluded. And so it went.

Not surprisingly, Richard graduated near the top of his class and was admitted to the business school of his choice. It was Professor McCormick who, during commencement, had the pleasure of awarding him a citation for academic distinction. And it was she who bet her colleagues that while Richard would do well in graduate school, he wouldn't rise to the top in the business world because he'd never test himself against the toughest standards—though if he did, she was equally convinced, he could meet them.

What To Do: Listen and Observe!

Listening and observing—that is, learning—is active, not passive, work. It's also demanding. To learn anything, you have to focus your attention. You have to fix your ears, eyes, and mind on what is before you. Most of us see and hear simply by being awake. But when you are really trying to learn, you must transform mere seeing and hearing into conscious efforts with all the energy you can bring to those tasks. For you learn not just by hearing what others say but by listening attentively to what they're saying, not just by looking at what others do but by observing intently what they're doing.

✔ *Accept nothing passively, absorb everything actively.* Inertia is no method. To learn, you must wrestle with everything you're exposed to, never letting it escape your attention. In that way, what you learn becomes your possession.

✔ *Listen to and observe those who teach you as if you were talking with them.* Don't just sit back and take notes on what they say. Instead, carry on silent conversations with them. What do his comments really signify? What does she mean by that?

✔ *Integrate what you observe and hear into what you already know.* This gives pieces of information their "roots" in the soil of knowledge you already possess; otherwise, they're just loose seeds falling on rocks, likely to be blown away by the first wind.

3

Enthusiasm

Granted, the work of learning is hard for most people. Granted, much of it is no fun. But there are ways to make it easier and more satisfying than you might imagine, provided that you develop some of the qualities that can make it so. One of those ways is to become enthusiastic about learning, so that you find it interesting, stimulating, and even entertaining. And that requires particular, possibly new, ways of looking at what you're going through.

Despite its intrinsic difficulty, learning is like love. Just as there has to be some magnetism, some mystery, between you and a loved one before you want to spend time with that person, so you have to feel an attraction for a topic, a subject, or a problem before you can learn about it.

Something has to draw you toward what you're supposed to learn—perhaps your own curiosity to find out more about a subject, or the subject's particular fascination for you, or the urging of someone you respect that you learn more about it. Maybe you grasp the subject's importance. Maybe you understand that knowing it will benefit you in some way.

Possibly you simply find it interesting. But without a doubt, if that "something" isn't there, if you don't have a passion of some sort, you'd better try to manufacture it if you want to get the most out of studying. Sometimes we hate a subject. We resent being forced to study something we detest; we loathe going to school, and we want

Learning in Spite of a Bad Teacher

Most teachers try to be interesting and helpful. Most retain their enthusiasm for the subjects they teach and are able to communicate their enthusiasm and knowledge to you. But there are inept teachers who appear, like some students, to be fish out of water in the classroom, who appear to know nothing about their subjects, or who are incapable of communicating what they know to you. What should you do if you find yourself in the class of such a teacher?

First, avoid doing what you shouldn't do. Setting off fireworks under a bad teacher's car or leading a protest march on the school grounds with signs urging that he be fired is likely to get you in trouble. Anyway, such actions won't help you to learn the subject he's supposed to be teaching. And that is, after all, why you're studying.

Act first to protect your own interests. When faced with a bad teacher, you will probably have to rely more on your textbooks and on other books about the subject. You'll need to go off on your own and find out what the subject holds, learn as much about it as you can by yourself, seek the help of other teachers (and librarians, too), and, reconciling yourself to your temporary bad fortune, get as much out of the situation as you can.

Rely on classmates for support and help. Rather than complaining with them, try studying with them and exchanging ideas and knowledge with them—good ways to make up for any deficiencies in your teachers. You need to build and furnish your own room in the house of learning. What you make for yourself is bound to be more interesting to you than anything built by others.

Above all, try to maintain a positive attitude, even if you have the Devil himself for an instructor. It's a mistake to think that you can punish an ineffective teacher by neglecting your own interests. Poor teachers aren't interested in the success or failure of their students, and so they're largely insensitive to anything you try or fail to do. So please yourself, not them.

to get out of the classroom at all costs. That's not unusual. But remaining in that state of mind for very long has serious consequences —wasted opportunities that may not return, failure to keep up in class, cynicism about learning anything, or a desire to stop learning altogether.

What should you do in such a predicament? How do you endeavor to find something of interest, perhaps something that deeply appeals to you or attracts your intellect, in a course you can't stand or at a time in your life when you'd prefer to be doing anything but studying? How can you understand your situation well enough to make something good out of what seems to be a bad deal?

As with most matters in life, there are no simple answers to these questions. The easiest solution lies in teachers who will fascinate you with their subjects in spite of your initial repugnance and lead you happily along the path to knowledge. Maybe you'll be lucky enough to find such spellbinders who can teach you without exertion on your part. Or maybe a bolt of lightning out of the blue will transform you into a passionate and devoted enthusiast of a subject you thought you hated; that way, you won't have to struggle so much.

But as the old saying has it, if wishes were horses, beggars would ride. Rather than waiting for a miracle, you'd better try to take charge of your own situation. That's probably the quickest way for anything to change for the better. You are the one who has to figure out how to create some interest in—and, if you're lucky, some genuine enthusiasm for—something you're stuck with in any case.

■

You may dispute our assertion that you're not likely to learn anything without having some desire to learn it. Clearly, some of life's practical lessons can be learned involuntarily. Children quickly discover that fire burns and causes pain. But you suffer no such immediate or physical consequences if you lack a burning desire to learn algebra. Your ignorance of the subject causes you no immediate harm. Apart from a poor grade, coasting through algebra may not affect your life directly. You're not likely to lose friends, do badly on the tennis court, or fail to get a summer job. Only down the road, when it's hard to backtrack and when delayed regret must substitute for close-up satisfaction, will the damage from your failure to learn algebra— say, to your reasoning abilities, or to your understanding of finance— begin to surface.

It helps to remember that all students have been in your shoes at one time or another. And most have probably found out what you're now facing—that manufacturing enthusiasm for something you don't like is a much tougher assignment than learning something you enjoy.

This is not to say, however, that you have to struggle all alone and without help to find some interest in every subject. Your teachers will help you; but few of them are mind readers, and many of them, especially your college professors, believe that you'll learn best if you, and not they, take the initiative in seeking their aid. Most teachers like to be asked for assistance, though it helps to approach them at a good time. A professor of theology, running to catch a bus, was waylaid by one of his students. "I know you haven't much time, professor," spluttered the student as he caught up with his teacher. "But I do have two quick questions about your course: what's the meaning of life, and is there a God?" Good questions, bad timing. Our out-of-breath student was so intent on finding the answers he needed that he abandoned tact, consideration, and common sense in his eager pursuit of them.

■

Who's to say what occasions such enthusiasm? Perhaps it's something in the subject itself or in the student. Enthusiasm for anything is often as mysterious to the enthusiast as it is to an onlooker. Why do some people enjoy watching ballet or listening to the opera? Why does the study of physics attract her? Why does marine biology interest him?

Perhaps a subject appeals to your aesthetic sense, perhaps to your desire for order. Perhaps you like physics because it explains how the material world works, while your friend likes it because it involves mathematics. If an ancestor fought in the Civil War, that period of history might fascinate you. You might feel a personal stake in it, so you couldn't find it boring. A possible result? You gain great pleasure from learning about it because you're also learning something about yourself.

How can you create such interest in the subjects you're studying, or even develop an interest in studying itself?

✔ *Success in learning anything is likely to be a source of satisfaction.* You rarely hear it said that learning can offer all sorts of pleasures. It's as if, to earn its claim to seriousness, studying should be like eating a lemon—bitter and hard to swallow. Some studying and some of what you study is truly boring, no doubt about it. "Much study is a weariness of the flesh," the Bible reminds us. For most of us there's not much pleasure in sitting for hours memorizing the principal parts of irregular Latin verbs. And much of what you learn about history —such as the lives lost in battles, the suffering of hungry people, and the costs of prejudice—causes pain rather than pleasure. But learning must have given some kind of pleasure to millions of others, or there wouldn't be so much knowledge in the world or so many people engaged in trying to create more knowledge. People didn't invent computers, find ways to save the environment, or articulate human experience in literature without some enthusiasm about these sometimes fiendishly difficult endeavors.

✔ *Enthusiasm begins with your own interests.* Your first step is to work hard to discover something about the subjects you're studying that might interest you. If you can't stand chemistry—learning symbols and equations, running experiments, writing up lab reports—you might look for something in the subject that reminds you of something else, like the magic tricks you enjoy performing. You can learn something about both magic and chemistry by comparing people's reactions to seeing the results of a chemical experiment and seeing a rabbit pulled from an empty hat.

✔ *Enthusiasm means letting favorites lead the way.* The subjects you find the most attractive are the ones that appeal to your own strengths and preferences. This means, of course, that you have to try even harder with the subjects that appeal to you the least. Given the diversity of subject matter and teaching styles you encounter in school and college, it shouldn't be too difficult to find some subjects and some teachers to fire you with enthusiasm. You may like your English teacher better than the one in chemistry, and on the whole you may prefer history to any other subject. So if you have any chance to choose, you should opt for the subjects and teachers that attract you the most. Having preferences means that you have interests—we all do. Acting on them will make you a better student. Your pleasures may vary from teacher to teacher and class to class, but at least you'll have some pleasures to work with.

✔ *Enthusiasm grows by connecting what you're learning with your life.* There's a danger in this, of course. People who insist that everything has to relate to them are often unduly self-centered. You don't want to go too far and conclude that what others know is of no consequence because it has no relation to you. Your experience of life is necessarily limited, and education is supposed to help you widen that experience. But if you can find something in a subject that might be of use, even if you don't like learning it, you will probably learn it more easily and remember it better. You'll eventually learn that some knowledge is wonderful simply because it exists and that learning can be its own reward. But much learning gains in strength and permanence by having a link to you—a link, however, that you must forge for yourself.

✔ *It's preferable to appeal to, rather than work against, your teachers.* The enthusiasm you display for a subject tends to confer another benefit on you: it improves the quality of your teachers' instruction. Teachers derive much of the vitality they need to sustain their demanding work from your own interests, drive, and aspiration. The freshness of your enthusiasm can save them from the boredom of an infinitely reiterated series of lessons. Teachers don't ask for, and shouldn't need, brilliant students to find delight in their efforts. What they do need is a sign (say, in the questions you ask) that they're reaching you and that you enjoy what you're learning or the process of learning itself—something within everyone's capacity. The house of learning has many rooms, and it's up to you to find your favorite ones and to spend some time there.

Most people are enthusiastic about something. No doubt you are, too. The trick is to link your enthusiasms with what you're required to study. That's not always easy. Sometimes your interests have nothing to do with the courses you take and the assignments you must complete. Yet learning and studying are made infinitely easier and more pleasant when you can figure out a way to give what you have to learn some relevance to what already arouses your interest.

Like so much else involved in learning, of course, finding that relevance sometimes demands that you bring it into existence yourself. You're not likely to find it by waiting for it to appear, like a change in the weather. But when you succeed in linking what is required of you to your own enthusiasms, you'll find that learning and studying become easier, more satisfying, and, most important, more lasting.

Archie Smith was the most apathetic student in his school. By the time he entered ninth grade, he'd already dropped a year behind because he had spent two years in the seventh grade. (Not that repeating a grade had done him any good.) His sole pleasures were his bus rides to and from home and his lunch recesses—the times when no one asked him to think. As if that weren't bad enough, he actually liked cafeteria food, probably because he couldn't be bothered to imagine an alternative. His teachers never saw him smile or show an interest in anything they said or did, and they couldn't interest him even in seeking help for his problem.

The favorite term in Archie's vocabulary was "boring." To him, everything was boring, even the hours he spent staring vacantly at the television screen at home. The pounding of rock music on his headphones saved him from total boredom because it prevented him from thinking about how boring everything else was. In fact, the headphones were as much a part of him as his scalp, and he would have resisted the removal of either with the same force.

Archie was not the kind of student his teachers wanted to teach. Some tried to get him to pay more attention in class by placing him in the front row. But eventually they gave up and let him drift to the back of the room, where he could avoid drawing attention to himself by pretending to sleep most of the time. Archie was not going to make any effort to gratify them. He never worked on the assignments they handed out. "Who wants to do this stuff?" he'd ask. His papers, written with minimum effort, always came in on time, but only because he knew the reward of punctuality: it would guarantee a D for effort, while an F for lateness would cause more boring work.

Although Archie wanted to have close friends, he didn't. He resented students who found their schoolwork interesting, who chatted and laughed easily with their teachers, and who got good grades. He explained their fortune to himself by rationalizing that they were "teachers' pets," and that was why, he grumbled, they received good report cards. He became especially angry when classmates suggested that he might like to read something funny in their history text or in a short story in their literature anthology. "These people must be crazy to suggest something so stupid and boring," he'd think. Even those who'd been his friends from elementary school began to shun him. "Archie's weird," they'd tell each other. "And besides, he's so boring!"

Yet despite Archie's indifference to the world around him, he sensed that something was wrong with his life. Other people seemed to learn. Many enjoyed doing so. And a few tried occasionally to show him how a subject could be interesting—or at least why they found it so. When this happened, he felt mildly guilty that he couldn't summon up any interest in anything; he knew that they hoped for at least a lukewarm response and were disappointed when he failed altogether to repay their efforts. Perhaps there was something wrong with him, something that prevented him from having friends or sharing others' interests. He tolerated their good-natured kidding— "Come on, Archie, it really isn't that boring, you know." Or, "Here's a guy who makes a 'couch potato' look like a star athlete." He smiled lamely back at them, as if grateful for any kind of attention.

Archie's only goal was to escape from the present and all

the stupidity and boredom it brought. But where would he escape to? He had no concept of the future other than getting away from the present. Why go to school? he asked himself. After all, his parents didn't know Latin, but they had good jobs. They didn't need to learn how to dissect frogs in order to make money. Did people think that reading Shakespeare's plays or being able to explain the difference between an adverb and an adjective had helped them buy a great new car? Because he knew he wasn't required to go to school after the twelfth grade, he planned to hang on until then with little effort and much boredom.

And he did so, although nothing could rouse Archie from his torpor or relieve his tedium in the meantime. Graduating from high school by the skin of his teeth, he had no idea what to do. When someone offered him a job, he took it. His job? Cleaning fish for a supermarket chain. Boring and smelly, he complained. His acquaintances agreed—the first time they'd agreed with any of his views for a long time.

What To Do: Reflect!

Reflecting on what you're learning is a sure way to make it your own. It also helps you remember it, because reflection allows you to integrate what you are learning into what you already know. Whenever you ask yourself "How does this affect what I learned yesterday?" or whenever you say to yourself "Given what I already know, that simply doesn't make sense," you're involved in reflection.

✔ *Think of reflection as a kind of disciplined daydreaming.* Let your mind wander, but along paths you direct it to take. If it wanders aimlessly, it is not serving its function as a doubter, evaluator, and critic.

✔ *Ask questions about what you're learning and what you know.* There's no better ignition to reflection than an interrogative. "Why is that so?" "What does that mean?" "How does that relate to what I've already learned?"

✔ *Seek the significance of everything you learn.* Never forget to ask what difference what you've just learned makes—to its subject, to others, and to you. "Why does anyone want to know that?" and "What does this mean?" are tough questions. But they're honest and effective, and thoughtful answers to them lead to greater understanding.

✔ *Remember that understanding comes only from you.* Meaning is inherent in nothing. To understand something you must reflect upon it. Until you do that, it's nothing but inert information, scarcely worth bothering to acquire.

Pleasure

Because it takes hard work to learn, studying can temporarily drain all pleasure from your life. If you take it seriously, it keeps you from your friends and other activities for the time you're engaged in it. And it's frustrating. Sometimes you can't figure out why you're being put through the torture. After all, why should you study French or biology, math or history, when you don't plan to use any one of those subjects after you graduate? Why are you going through all this "wasted" effort?

You're doing so because studying and learning can bring you all sorts of unexpected satisfactions if you consider them in the way that is most relevant to the nature of knowledge itself. For the pleasures of learning and understanding are not always immediate, and they're rarely the pleasures you feel when something makes you laugh uncontrollably or when you're being entertained by friends. The pleasures of learning are more subtle than that, more distinctive, more internal, and more long-lasting—and different from the ones you usually seek. They're quiet, special satisfactions, the ones you savor long after you've forgotten their sources and the occasions in which you gained the knowledge that sustains them.

Also, the pleasures of learning are individual. What

you enjoy learning and knowing may not be what your friends enjoy. Don't be surprised if you take pleasure in a subject that bores others to tears and if you occasionally feel obliged to keep that pleasure to yourself out of a fear of others' ridicule or incredulity. You're under no obligation to like what others like or to detest what they hate, any more than you should expect their tastes and pleasures in, say, food or movies to match your own. Just as you have to follow the song in your own heart when you learn, so you have to be prepared to find satisfactions in learning that are yours alone.

Learning and knowing don't yield only serious pleasures. On the contrary. Your classrooms and desks should be places of light hearts as well as serious minds. There's a large place in learning for laughter, wit, and jokes. And by their very nature, these kinds of pleasures are shared pleasures. Although what you find pleasing may not please everyone else, you'll often join others to laugh at the same jokes, or the same absurdities. Without such a general recognition of what's funny, writers of comedy wouldn't be able to make the majority of us laugh with such reliable regularity. In fact, to be able to understand a joke at all, you have to be "in the know," for one of the components of all humor, wherever you can find it, is knowledge.

So if home and workplace provide many opportunities for good laughs now and then, shouldn't the classroom, too? You need as many, perhaps more, light moments of relaxed enjoyment there if you're to sustain the necessary application of your attention to the work of learning.

In the best sense of the word, then, learning should be play as well as work—the play of people and ideas with one another. To be sure, it's often serious play, as when young children become absorbed in the games they play. Play isn't the absence of seriousness. Instead, it is delight in the unexpected, the sudden recognition of beauty and truth, the understanding that shines out of wit. It's also playing off one argument against another and playing around with ideas and knowledge as they evolve.

But the greatest pleasures that come from studying and learning are particular and different. They're not sudden bursts of

Delayed Gratification

Everyone wants immediate payoffs.

After putting in a full day of classes and study, you want to take the test the next day, get an A on it, and then be able to forget what you've just mastered. Or you're annoyed by the required course on Shakespeare because you're a business major, and the course doesn't contribute directly to your plans to start a computer company when you graduate.

These are natural objections, and they deserve answers. But they may not be the kinds of answers you like or want, because they require an act of faith on your part, which is where the problem begins: you want visible and immediate results, not ones that require trust in beneficial and general results in an unseen future.

Just as you strengthen your muscles because to do so improves your well-being, and then, all of a sudden, you discover that strong arms are useful in playing tennis, so you learn history and math without having any specific use for either and then find, to your surprise, that your ability to understand presidential elections or to reason in an organized fashion has benefited from what you learned some years ago. In other words, you often learn subjects and develop abilities that have general, rather than specific, applicability so that you quicken and strengthen your general capacities—in this case the capacity to think strongly and well.

In addition, you postpone immediate gratification

—you study for your science course rather than going to the movies with friends—because of the greater good you can do for yourself in the future by doing hard and unpleasant work now. Perhaps that greater good will come in the form of better grades and therefore a better chance to get into a college or graduate school of your choice. Perhaps it will come in the form of deeper understanding of science in general, so that you'll be a better-informed citizen. Those prospective results are positive consequences of your faith in the possibility of a benefit somewhere down the road.

As the nineteenth-century Danish existentialist philosopher Søren Kierkegaard once remarked, "Life is lived forward, but it is understood backward." You never know how, when, or why what you learn when you're young (much of it against your will) will affect your life, but it will always affect it, and almost always for the better. That's why you postpone immediate gratification—so that you have greater and longer-lasting gratification later.

pleasing sensation, like your first kiss. They don't originate in cynicism or the criticism of others' arguments and work. Instead, the greatest pleasures of studying and learning are tranquil and private ones. You feel them in your heart. Often, they're unexpected satisfactions. And while you can explain them to others, you can't share the feelings they cause. They're yours alone.

The principal pleasures you get from studying come from your own activity, from what you bring to your work. You must try to entertain yourself with the challenge and excitement of learning. You are the actor and the contestant, not the spectator. Nor are your teachers employed as entertainers. Their job requires that they engage you in mental activity, not hand you knowledge like a gift so that you can learn—or think you're learning—without effort.

Yet given the competition from the visual media all around you—television and computers in particular—your teachers are in a tough spot. You're accustomed to special effects and to rapid stimuli. Your teachers can rarely provide provocative fare that matches these. They may have CD-ROMs and lively visual aids, or they may be armed only with a piece of chalk in one hand and a book in the other. But whatever your teachers have to inspire your curiosity, to make their efforts interesting, even exciting, you have to invest heavily of your own will and imagination in the work you're engaged in. If you sit inertly, waiting to be dazzled with lights, movement, music, and drama, you'll be bored to distraction within minutes.

Is it really possible that your active participation can bring pleasure into your school and college days? The odds may seem unfavorable, especially when learning is compared with such activities as going to the movies. Yet while movies may be exciting, they're somebody else's concept, brainchild, and production. By contrast, what you learn and know is your own because of the activity you put into it. What you learn contributes to your own identity, determines who you are as a person, and gives you the capacity to understand a part of the world. That's the satisfaction and pleasure you can look forward to by learning something.

What's more, all the special effects of the media are nothing compared with the satisfactions that come from your own active engagement in what you are learning. Knowledge is an enduring reality; what comes from outside is often an artificial and passing illusion, no matter how persuasive and seductive its momentary attraction. If, as is said, possession is nine points of the law, it's also nine-tenths of pleasure. What you have and hold, what nobody can take away from you: that's what's really worth possessing.

■

When you walk down the corridor toward a class, are you thinking, "This is going to be a great class! A whole hour of Mr. Blank-insop and his molecules!" Or is your first thought, "Here comes another everlasting hour of unrelieved tedium for me, the sacrificial victim on the altar of education and parental aspiration"? Like beauty, learning is in the eye of the beholder. And so it helps to wear the right mental glasses—to prepare yourself as best you can to take in what you have to study anyway.

One of the tricks of making tough classroom work more pleasant and satisfying is to concentrate on the moments when the tedium lifts. (It always does, we promise.) Whatever the subject, somebody gets excited about it, as you no doubt can, too. Maybe someone will make a statement or ask a question that strikes a chord. When that happens, you can't push the subject away. Instead, you embrace it. You try to take it into your mind as completely as you can. Who knows? It may find its way into your heart as well. Before you know it, chemistry may be your greatest delight, and the introductory course in sociology your favorite place to be with friends. Once you learn to give a fair chance to everything you're studying and trying to learn, you'll begin to earn dividends of pleasure and satisfaction that you couldn't have imagined before.

So what can we conclude about the satisfactions of learning?

✔ *The pleasures of learning often require that you postpone immediate pleasures.* That's not to say that learning never brings bursts of satisfaction or joy; it often does. But sitting down to study with a book, a notepad, and a pen may not always generate sensations of delight or excitement. Instead, the self-denial required for study, the giving up of immediate and intense pleasures, prepares you for delights of a subtler and less material kind. It's like climbing a mountain: doing so takes hours, maybe days, but you can't enjoy the view from the summit—to say nothing of the sheer satisfaction of having made it to the top—without struggling to get there. Similarly with the heroes and heroines of your favorite childhood stories—indeed, with the heroes and heroines of life itself: they can't avoid battles with hardship and unhappiness. Their success in overcoming obstacles and dangers is what makes them heroes to begin with.

✔ *The pleasures of study are often solitary.* A marooned sailor or a prisoner in solitary confinement isn't the likeliest candidate for happiness. But the challenges of lonely study can often contradict your expectations. The isolated souls of desert isles and the inmates of the most awful prisons have found sustaining purpose in absorbing activities—challenges or interests so intense that they could ignore where they were, so demanding that they considered the presence of anyone else as an intrusion. A few such people have used their forced solitude for extraordinary purposes. Consider how South Africa's Nelson Mandela spent his years in solitary confinement. He steeled himself against despair by observing as much of the world as he could in books and other publications in order to figure out how to transform his country's history. Study often requires, just as it often repays, such intensity of concentration. It is therefore useful to view solitary work as a condition favorable to learning. Then, when you make a breakthrough or discovery, you'll be able to share your excitement with others.

✔ *Gaining knowledge may demand effort, but ignorance brings misery.* Any time your education is too troublesome, consider its alternative—ignorance. Some people do succeed in life without knowledge, but they're so rare as to be remarkable. Nor is material success guaranteed by education—if it were, university professors would be the richest people in the world. Instead, it's the pleasures of awareness, understanding, and wisdom that are ensured by learning. We hear more these days about stupidity than about ignorance, but stupidity is often little more than the evidence of ignorance.

✔ *Charting your own journey to knowledge is the ulti-mate pleasure.* The eighteenth-century French philosopher Voltaire told us that "we must cultivate our garden." Voltaire wasn't urging us to be horticulturists. He meant that just as a particular garden plot has a certain soil and climate, so we have been allocated certain apti-tudes and talents for learning. Therefore just as skilled gardeners learn to grow vegetables and flowers in the environment given to them, it's up to you to develop your own potentialities to the greatest ad-vantage. Voltaire's admonition affirms the good sense of not envying somebody else's garden but instead devoting yourself to your own. Although other gardeners may be able to guide you because of their greater experience, ultimately only you can decide how your garden will be arranged and what you'll grow there. In other words, there's a limit to the helpfulness of teaching and advice, no matter how be-nevolent or wise it may be. Learning must be your own creation— and therefore your own satisfaction.

Much learning yields its pleasures down the road to knowl-edge, not right away; and much learning gives satisfaction long after the tough work of studying is over. Moreover, most of the satisfac-tions that come with understanding fit the nature of learning itself: they're sober satisfactions, not uproarious ones—and no doubt, con-sequently, sustained and memorable. They're the kinds that result in pride in what you've achieved and that yield the praises of your real friends, of your parents, and of those you respect the most.

They are also the kinds of satisfactions you have to seek on your own. They're not the kind delivered to passive spectators in a movie theater or at a sports event, where you can sit back and en-joy what others have prepared for you. Instead, they result from your engagement with your studies and from your efforts to give meaning to what you're coming to know and understand. Those self-created satisfactions are the best that life can offer.

Deirdre O'Greann was a junior in high school, a popular young woman with an infectious laugh. She could find some pleasure in most activities, but she had no particular relish for any of her classes. This worried her because SATs were coming up, and the college of her choice rarely accepted anyone with scores below the seven hundreds.

She shared her concern one day with her favorite aunt. "If I could find something about my classes I liked," Deirdre told her, "I think I'd be able to study more and do better, but I can't seem to find it."

"Tell you what," said her aunt. "You tell me what you enjoy the most, and I'll tell you how to relate it to your schoolwork."

"You know I really like acting," Deirdre replied. "I like pretending to be someone else."

"Then you should do some acting to help you in school," her aunt suggested. "And you should probably impersonate a student who's really engaged in the subjects she's studying, someone who enjoys everything about her classes."

"But I'd feel like a complete fraud," Deirdre protested.

"Nonsense!" said her aunt. "You play parts on stage without complaining that you're a fraud. I saw you in *Our Town* last year, remember? And this is more important than a play. You're going to try to act the part of a person who enjoys learning."

After more protests, Deirdre finally agreed to try out her aunt's idea, not because she really wanted to but because she had faith in her aunt's wisdom. Besides, she was desperate enough to try anything that might help her in school.

But what was she to do, especially in French and biology, for which she had no enthusiasm? She and her aunt decided that she should become a hand raiser and questioner—a role she'd never played, preferring to sit quietly and let everyone else do the talking.

To play the role well, she had to do three other things, too. First, she had to work her way into the role by imagining herself volunteering questions in class, just as she had to assume the characters of the parts she played on stage. Second, she had to practice asking questions, which she did (feeling silly) in front of a mirror. Third, she had to study the subjects well enough to ask intelligent questions about them, just as she had to memorize her lines in plays.

After asking a question on the first day of her experiment—the lesson was about mammals, and she felt a kind of stage fright before she raised her hand—she got an answer that she didn't expect or want. Deirdre's teacher gave a brief answer, then said, "That's a tough question. See me after class and we'll discuss it further." Maybe I should change roles, Deirdre thought to herself.

But contrary to her fears, her chat with her teacher—the first she'd ever had—was pleasant, even fun, almost like two old friends with a common interest. Deirdre came away from it with a book on mammals that her teacher thought she might find interesting. She had to read it, of course, so that she could return it with a few thoughtful comments. But even that wasn't as much of a chore as she feared. She actually enjoyed the book.

It was much the same with French. After she had asked some questions in that course, her teacher, taking serious note of her for the first time, persuaded her to accept the job of helping to arrange a class trip to Montreal. Deirdre found herself spending more time perfecting her French so that she could understand what she had to read to help plan the trip.

By the time she was three weeks into this kind of playacting, all new to her, Deirdre found herself much busier with all her courses and, what was more interesting to her, beginning to feel some genuine pleasure in them. More direct involvement with her teachers was something she found she liked, and the more intensive study she'd had to undertake gave her a taste for a couple of subjects that she hadn't liked previously but on which she'd now become something of a minor expert. And all by having adopted some new and simple approaches to learning anything.

Her aunt, who had known all along that this was likely to happen, took quiet satisfaction in her own role in Deirdre's newfound pleasure. When Deirdre told her that she no longer had to act in order to appear to be enjoying her studies because now she actually enjoyed them, her aunt laughed. "Of course you don't. I was just typecasting you when I suggested that you try it. But see how important it is to enjoy what you're learning, even if at first you have to indulge in a bit of make-believe?"

What To Do: Question!

Failing to ask questions is a sure road to ignorance and error. If you accept everything as it is told to you, your mind becomes lazy and you become dependent on others for thinking and knowledge. You should avoid that at all costs.

✔ *Why? should be your most frequent question.* Always seek explanations. Never take anything at face value. Get to the root of things. A student without "whys?" can never be wise, and the lamp of knowledge will surely go out if the "whattage" is too low.

✔ *Never stop asking yourself: what questions should I be asking?* Questions don't just exist, as air does. You have to provide them. The most important of all questions, "What should I ask?" is the key to all learning.

✔ *Don't take any answer on faith.* Seek answers from others, especially your teachers, but don't rely entirely on them. They may know their subjects thoroughly; they may understand their own minds. But your mind is yours alone, and it's you who must be convinced.

✔ *Seek an explanation for everything.* Hard work? Never-ending? Yes. But when you have sought and received an explanation for something, you'll comprehend it more thoroughly, accept it more willingly, and remember it more fully.

5

. . . .

Curiosity

"Four be the things I'd been better without," wrote the notorious wit Dorothy Parker in an example of bad verse. "Love, curiosity, freckles, and doubt." But she was wrong on all counts, even, we're confident, about the freckles. Freckles and love may have gotten Parker into trouble now and then, but for a student those other qualities, doubt and curiosity, do the opposite. You can't be without them. They're your intellectual and spiritual oxygen.

Your natural appetite to find out about the world can get you to consume mountains of facts. It can unfold the meanings of the world's many mysteries and steer you toward an understanding of life in all its dimensions—if you indulge it. And curiosity helps you to work hard and apply self-discipline, other qualities you need to become the best student you can be.

Curiosity's virtue is its greed. It wonders, often indiscriminately, about everything it focuses on. Curiosity carries you, limited by time and space, beyond the immediate. It knows no boundaries, and it pushes you to learn about everything that's still unknown or unfamiliar to you. It can as easily direct itself to the ancient Egyptians as to the wriggling pond-life under your microscope. But that's also its vice, for it's usually directed to very particular interests—say, to ballet or to bugs. You therefore have to make strenuous efforts to extend its range, so that your wonder about ballet becomes knowledge about dance, or so that your fascination with bugs turns into a lifelong love affair with the entire natural world.

When you were a child, your eagerness to learn defined your behavior. You were full of wonder about everything—touching, holding, maybe wrecking anything that came into your reach. And as soon as you could talk you were full of questions: why is the sky blue? why is up up? why can't tomorrow be yesterday? You found everything "curiouser and curiouser," as Alice found it in Wonderland. Adults tried to answer your endless questions (even if you sometimes drove them crazy with them), for they knew that by rewarding your natural inquisitiveness and by satisfying your excitement to know, they'd help you to learn and, equally important, to acquire a taste for learning throughout your life.

But three changes probably occurred in you as you grew older. Your sense of wonder began to be affected by your growing understanding of the realities of the world. What earlier may have appeared wonderful and full of mystery began to seem routine and commonplace. In addition, other people gradually turned over to you the task of satisfying your curiosity. They made it clear that you were now on your own to learn, whether about airplanes or the trombone, and you quickly discovered that learning required work, which you preferred to avoid.

Finally, you probably became self-conscious about your curiosity (just as you did about everything else) and began to fear asking questions publicly. You were even afraid to ask questions of the teachers who most welcomed your raised hand and your "I don't get it." You also feared that to appear to have some passionate interest that others didn't possess was to expose your ignorance to others (as if they knew everything) or to make yourself the victim of their scorn for what you wanted to know about (as if others' interests should be yours). So there's a good chance that you stopped asking questions and shut up like a clam.

But curiosity can be every student's best friend. It's the inner signal of what your mind and spirit want to know at any particular time. Because it often springs up unexpectedly—quietly insisting

What Is Knowledge?

You ask questions and pursue your curiosity for a single reason: to create knowledge.

Yet you must keep this in mind about knowledge: it isn't the same thing as information. Knowledge is information that has been given organization, meaning, and use. Facts exist by themselves. Knowledge is a human creation.

The Declaration of Independence was made public to the world on July 4, 1776. That's a fact—information related to nothing else. The Declaration's meaning and significance for history—its centrality to the public philosophy of the United States, the way it has become key to advances in civil rights and liberties—constitute knowledge.

Hydrogen and chlorine are elements of nature. That's a fact. Your understanding that, when combined, these two elements create new substances, such as hydrochloric acid, which has certain characteristics that hydrogen and chlorine independently don't have, constitutes knowledge.

Knowledge differs from information as music differs from sound. An orchestra warming up doesn't make music; it makes only noise. It makes music when the conductor takes over and each performer follows the score in

cooperation with one another. Music is sound given form
and significance.

Similarly, knowledge is information given structure
and meaning. The facts in your head become knowledge
when you put them together so that they're related to one
another and, put together, take on meaning that is larger
than the mere facts alone.

Nothing has meaning by itself. Information has to
gain meaning from the application of human thought. To
attain knowledge, you must struggle endlessly to derive
meaning from information.

that you want to know this or to get the answer to that—it tells you
something about your own bewildering, particular self. It's a guide
to the way your mind works, the origin of every inquiry you launch
and of every discovery you make. And like all good friends, you can
follow its guidance with confidence.

Yet curiosity makes demands on you. If you're to benefit
from it, you must act on its summons, for it often knows better than
you what is best for you. You must also sometimes manufacture curiosity, for while it's possible to force yourself to master something
that deeply bores you, you can often cultivate curiosity by getting
ahead of it—by stumbling upon something interesting without knowing that it will interest you and then becoming curious to learn more
about it. Curiosity is hard to control; it can be insatiable. But without
it, you miss what might spur you on to learn more.

It's easy enough to respond to the spur of curiosity. But it's
much harder to generate curiosity when it isn't there. You can't force
yourself to be interested in something. The trick is to lie in ambush
for curiosity. You've got to try to be attentive to everything you study
and learn, to range widely throughout the world of knowledge, and
then to pounce on something that happens to rouse your interest—

to try to answer your sudden torrent of questions as soon as they appear, even if you have neither time nor energy to pursue them all. In this way, curiosity is a bit like conscience: it doesn't let you alone, and it's better followed than avoided.

■

Unlike conscience, which attaches itself to the same concerns in most of us, curiosity is, like imagination and aspiration, an individual quality. Just as each of us differs from others in size and shape, so each of us is curious about different topics. Just as there are different kinds of mental and creative skills, so each mind is provoked to wonder about different subjects. You may be fascinated by mathematical logic, while your musical friend can't figure out why you're not astonished by the qualities of sixteenth notes.

Such vast differences in natural interests justify the confusing abundance of courses that schools and colleges offer. Although some people criticize educational institutions for overindulging their students with countless specialized courses, the difficult choices you must make among them result from students' desires to learn about more and more subjects.

Yet the difficulty you may experience in choosing between too many courses points to a genuine problem with curiosity: as a student, you must learn to discipline it even as you yield to it. Because it is often indiscriminate, curiosity requires you to be selective—to choose among the many questions you may want to pursue, the many answers you may want to have. Having to select among the questions that crowd your mind and concentrate your energies and studies in pursuing only some of them is among the most necessary and daunting challenges you face.

In fact, curiosity is a virtue only in moderation. You have to make it work for you so that it doesn't overwhelm you in indiscriminate study and learning. You have to learn to become more conscious, practiced, and determined in your curiosity, your natural sense of wonder, for your own good as a student. How can you yield to curiosity, yet not too much?

✔ *To be curious, like a young child you have to open yourself to all experience.* You never know what you'll be curious about, or when or where you'll become curious about something, and you surely never know what you'll learn if you pursue your curiosity. So you should let the great unstoppable questions of life—why? what? who? when?—flood your mind. After all, if you don't ask these questions, you can't answer them; and if you don't at least try to answer them, you don't learn. You may think that teachers like to ask all the questions. Not so. They like you to ask your own. And haven't you noticed that your questions are almost always more interesting and productive than those others ask?

✔ *Opening yourself to experience means yielding to your curiosity and then directing it.* Curiosity denied exacts its punishments—dissatisfaction with yourself and, worse, lost opportunities to learn. So it is essential to follow your own curiosity and give way to it at first. As every scientist and historian knows, what you can ask out of genuine ignorance, perplexity, and wonder, free of preconception and prejudice, most often yields the freshest and most fascinating answers. And those answers will most likely become a permanent part of your understanding of the world. Nevertheless, at some point you have to direct your interests in the world, confine your search, and decide what you're going to let yourself pursue. This isn't an injunction to specialize. Instead, it's advice to make hard choices as to how you are going to use your precious time as a student.

✔ *Curiosity kindles curiosity.* The mysterious, internal workings of curiosity and wonder push us to detective work, in which each clue leads to another and each fact leads to additional questions. Even when the mystery has been solved and the criminal unmasked, often you still don't know whether he's the only one, or whether you understand his motive, or whether the solution to his crime makes sense. You're left with still more questions. And so it is with curiosity. It pushes you endlessly; it makes you forever a student. And so you grow in knowledge and understanding.

✔   *The absence of curiosity shouldn't make you hopeless.* Lacking curiosity doesn't mean that your brain's gone dead. Instead, it's likely to mean that you're not paying enough attention to the world around you, or that you're concentrating on one or two passive or nonproductive activities, like television watching, to the exclusion of everything else. It's therefore probably a good idea to turn off the TV or unplug the headphones and look for something new.

✔   *Frustrated curiosity can be creative.* Sometimes you can't find answers to satisfy your curiosity. In those cases, you can learn from the very fact that you can't satisfy it. Perhaps you haven't tried hard enough; perhaps you haven't looked in the right places. If no one has yet answered the question that's puzzling you, then you may be the first to do so. Knowing or doing what no one has previously figured out how to know or do is the basis of all discoveries, inventions, and new ideas.

✔   *The entire world can satisfy, as well as arouse, your curiosity, if only you use it.* People are not the only source of answers to your questions. So are books, works of art and music, and institutions like libraries and museums, which contain knowledge and creative works. One advantage these sources have for the timid is that they don't dismiss you or laugh at you for the questions you ask. In fact, besides your teachers, your best friends as a student are likely to be librarians and museum guides—the unsung heroes of the world of learning. You can confide in them, ask them questions, depend on them. Their job, like your teachers', is to help you satisfy your curiosity.

As long as your mind is receptive to knowledge—and few minds aren't—you wonder about the world. You want to know about it, settle some doubt about it, or quiet some confusion in your mind. You ask yourself how an automobile engine works, what brush strokes a certain artist uses to achieve his effects, or why the planets don't fly off into space. Struck by the majesty of a mountain vista, you begin to wonder how the mountains rose, or why they rose in the distance and not at the spot where you're standing. You seek the answers from a teacher or a book, and soon you're off learning about geology. Or, moved by the beauty of a lyric poem, you read more of its author's work, then the works of other poets of the time, then about poetry and criticism of poetry; and soon you're knowledgeable about a major branch of literature.

Wondering about something means being open to knowledge and the possibility of surprise; it means letting yourself be puzzled or astonished by something new, strange, unknown, or not understood. Once you're puzzled or surprised, your curiosity is aroused. And if you follow that aroused curiosity, you're on the path toward knowledge.

The habit of wondering about everything is well worth the modest troubles it may cause you. The eighteenth-century British writer and eccentric wit Samuel Johnson (often known simply as Dr. Johnson) observed that curiosity "is one of the permanent and certain characteristics of a vigorous mind." Like the grains of sand inside an oyster's shell, little irritations of curiosity can produce pearls. So in the end, curiosity not only helps you become a better student but also spurs you to the active pursuit of the knowledge that constitutes true learning.

Bruce "The Tower" Byrd wasn't your average student. He was tall enough to be a basketball player—six feet eight in his socks—

but too scrawny and uncoordinated to be an athlete of any kind. His pronounced stoop, sharp nose, and thick glasses gave him the look of a near-sighted vulture. You could imagine smaller creatures scampering for cover whenever he loomed into view, even though he was no threat to anyone.

What really distinguished Bruce from his fellow students in their first year at the local community college was his insatiable interest in everything. He'd have been conspicuous anyway—his appearance guaranteed that. But his tendency to explore everything, query every statement, and grub around in the reference section of the library for the answers to every one of his innumerable questions set him apart from the flock.

Not that Bruce minded when others laughed at him. He appeared to be immune to their taunts. In fact, he seemed almost to enjoy them. When others made fun of him for charging around in search of answers to everything, he'd ask with a quizzical smile what was so strange about wanting to know something. "Aren't students supposed to be curious?" he'd wonder. The other students, if they answered at all, simply recited the familiar adage about curiosity killing the cat. They couldn't imagine themselves imitating his bizarre conduct. Asking questions? Sure—but just enough to get by.

First-year college biology is no snap for anyone, and Bruce's biology teacher was particularly tough—as well as serious and dry. During the students' first attempts at dissection, they did little more than name the principal body parts of the fish they were cutting up. But characteristically, Bruce had questions about the nervous system, muscular structure, and optical equipment of the fish. When his professor couldn't address Bruce's theorizing about how fish swim, he began to read so much about fish that he soon moved beyond his teacher's knowledge. He was especially interested in—and before long was especially knowledgeable about—diseases that could afflict fish and possibly the people who ate them. While other students dissected one specimen in their first class week, Bruce opened five, and his log of the questions he had asked and answered filled half a notebook.

By the second month of classes, his biology teacher realized that Bruce was a special kind of student. Even if Bruce sometimes inadvertently showed him up in front of the class by knowing more than he did, the professor saw that a career in scientific research was probably a good one for Bruce, and so he began to encourage Bruce to transfer to a four-year college with better laboratories that could prepare him for graduate school. The professor also expressed sympathy for Bruce when other students laughed because he was asking another question or volunteering another explanation. Obviously, they were laughing at Bruce's appearance and manner just as much as at his eagerness for knowledge, and that bothered the professor.

But Bruce told him that, as much as he appreciated his efforts, he understood why others laughed at him. "I've had a lot of experience with that," Bruce told him, "ever since the first grade, when I was already taller than everyone else. But they'd probably laugh at me even if I were the school's star running back. Even though they have shorter necks than mine, they don't want to stick theirs out."

After he got his college degree, Bruce graduated from medical school and began to pursue a cure for AIDS in a major research laboratory. His colleagues there seldom laugh at him. He's still known as "The Tower," but in that environment, they rely on him to ask the kinds of strange and demanding questions that can lead to medical breakthroughs, and they respect his ability to outdistance them with his far-ranging curiosity.

What To Do: Explore!

How do you know what may interest you or become an exciting addition to your knowledge unless you try learning about subjects about which you know nothing? Musicology? Sounds like some sort of disease, you say. Yet if you take up its study, you may become fascinated by the history and theory of music. You may study a subject and find it of no interest whatsoever. On the other hand, the subject may fascinate you and illuminate another subject you enjoy, and it will surely teach you something new about yourself or the world you live in.

✔ *Don't let your current knowledge and interests alone determine what you seek to learn.* Experiment. Expand your interests. There's no better time to do so than your years in school and college—when you have the most time, can receive the most encouragement, and have the most open mind.

✔ *Never think of a subject as useless.* So you'll never "use" mathematical logic, never "apply" knowledge of Renaissance art? At least you'll learn some logic, and then you'll understand what logicians do, why they do it, and what comes out of their work. And you'll never enter a museum and be as ignorant as you used to be about its treasures.

✔ *Choose your courses for their instructors as well as for their subjects.* When you are unsure about a subject, pick the most exciting teacher and take the subject on faith. You're not likely to be bored.

6

. . . .

Aspiration

It is always hard work to study and learn. But it's far more difficult to do so without a specific goal in mind—whether to achieve something never before achieved, to land a coveted career position, or to enter your chosen graduate program. If you just drift along, studying what's prescribed, without investing any of your own determination and hopes, you're unlikely to learn much or to get full benefit from the education you're being offered.

But simply having an objective in mind isn't enough. For there are all sorts of reasons for studying. You can study to get good grades, to please your parents, or to get into college or graduate school, but these aren't the best reasons for working hard in school or college. Such motivations have some benefits, but they don't satisfy your greatest long-term interests. If you decide to study because you want to learn about the world and your place in it, or because you want to achieve something with your life and to leave something enduring behind, you've found the best reasons to study, because they're linked to something estimable beyond yourself. They are the reasons that define aspiration.

Aspiration differs from ambition.

Many people will do anything for popularity, money, or power. Yet sometimes it's unclear why these people are pursuing these goals and doing so with such determination, frequently without

Don't Sell Yourself Short

Much is made these days of self-esteem. If you possess it, you are repeatedly told, your life will be more satisfying.

Yet a sense of self-worth is not something than can be given or taught to you. It has to come from within, and it has to be gained through your own achievements. It doesn't depend on what others think of you. Self-esteem is the sense you have of your own strengths and capacities. It's the sense you possess of your own attainments in learning and understanding.

Because evaluating your own strengths accurately is so difficult, it's easy to sell yourself short. (The opposite problem, of course, is having an inflated sense of your strengths.) Yet because so much of your sense of self develops in your student years, studying and learning are major means of gaining self-esteem. You learn about yourself by learning about others; and when you achieve understanding about something, you always experience the great satisfaction of feeling competent to know what you seek to know fully and well. But there are many potholes in the road to understanding—confusion, frustration, sometimes failure—and it's easy for you to lose faith in yourself, to think less of yourself than you should. How can you avoid doing so?

Don't evaluate yourself by others' standards. Set your own high, but reasonable, standards for learning. Then evaluate yourself against them. Setting appropriate standards can be difficult, so take your time in setting them. Seek the advice of others—parents, teachers, and friends—but rely in the end on what you and you alone know about yourself and your capabilities.

Insist on candid evaluations from others. Setting your own standards doesn't mean blindly ignoring all other judgments. Don't let anyone patronize you or let you off the hook by making you think your work better than it is. Press advisers for honesty, and prepare yourself for the disappointment and hurt you may momentarily feel when they respond honestly. Like the pain of an inoculation, that temporary pinprick will be to good purposes.

Develop reasonable goals, and then work hard to meet them. Here, the reasonableness is more important than the hard work. With sensible goals—what you decide you should learn in what amount of time, for example—you have a better chance of achieving what you set out to achieve. Unreasonable goals, whether set by yourself or others, too often lead to disappointment and a sense of incompetence. Chances are strong, however, that you're capable of attaining a reasonable goal.

concern for other people. Often these people seem to have no other aim than to win office or become rich—as if these were the keys to a happy and productive life. Many "famous" people aren't so much well-known as notorious; others are just "celebrities," in whom we're supposed to take an interest. But are they pursuing worthy ends with their lives, or are they interesting only because of their "lifestyles"? Are they merely famous for being famous?

The seventeenth-century Dutch philosopher Baruch Spinoza termed ambition "a species of madness." Ambition is not necessarily a bad quality, but in its true meaning it's a limited one. It suggests striving for a particular goal, but the word also connotes self-aggrandizement and self-promotion—benefit to self—rather than focus on the good of other people or on ideals. Ambition is a self-centered desire, often excessive and sometimes hurtful to others.

By contrast, aspiration is ambition linked to good purposes outside oneself, ambition linked to high ideals. Its satisfactions originate as much in the effort you put into something as in the achievement of giving something to the world. If the goals of aspiration aren't met, the disappointment doesn't feel like an injury to your self-esteem or honor. As the poet Robert Browning wrote,

> What I aspired to be,
> And was not, comforts me.

■

Not all ambition is unworthy. Surely, seeking to make a solid living, to use your skills for your benefit, or to make a name for yourself have their value and justifications; but these goals in themselves are of no necessary moral or ethical worth. They gain such worth only by the use to which they're put and by the meanings they come to possess—by the meanings you give them.

Why, then, is aspiration so important to your life as a student? Because it gives direction and value to all your hard work. Aspiration helps to organize your thinking, to sustain you when you're involved in the deepest and most frustrating struggles to put your mind to effective work. It helps you become what you are not yet but wish to be.

Yet aspiration is not easy to develop. It doesn't come to everyone, certainly not at the same time in life. It's often the fruit of sustained and mature reflection undertaken by virtue of experience, not always a quality you can develop when you're young. Yet once aspiration grips you with its intellectual adrenalin, you can perform feats of study and understanding well beyond your expectations.

Usually you must develop aspiration on your own. Few schools and colleges give high priority to fostering it, and most teachers and professors limit their responsibility to teaching you "subjects" rather than approaches to life. But the best of your teachers and professors try, usually more by the way they carry themselves than by direct statement, to persuade you that you are privileged to have the opportunity to study. Good teachers show you that it is your responsibility to use your education and the years of your life when you're in school and college for the good of others. They reveal to you that you have a responsibility to those who have taught and preceded you in the classroom to live up to the high standards and expectations that they've already marked out for you.

Too heavy a burden? We don't think so, because the aim of high standards, like everything else worthwhile in education, is to inspire you to surpass yourself—to stimulate your imagination so that you see yourself in other places, at other times, beyond the circumstances into which you were born. This is the hallmark of great schools, colleges, and universities as well as of great teachers—that they instill in you the aspiration to reach beyond your limited world and envision a good life for yourself and others. They want to see you reaching high.

You shouldn't expect to have aspiration naturally; nor should you expect others to create aspirations for you, any more than you can depend on others to make you work hard or to give you pleasure as a student. Any aspiration you have must be yours alone. If it's not, you're not going to be able to sustain it.

In this as in so many other cases, you have to give meaning to what you learn by reflecting long and hard about it. You can decide you want to be a biochemist because you like biochemistry and you hope for a position with a corporation that will employ your skills well. But wouldn't it be better to imagine putting your skills to use in trying to achieve what has never before been achieved, such as a cure for cancer or the means to clean up the world's store of toxic

wastes—and then seek a position, be it in a university or a corporation, that would encourage those ideals? If you're a talented artist,
you might envisage future employment in an advertising firm. But
couldn't you also strive to reach beyond the monetary rewards of that
kind of work and use your gifts to create works of true beauty and insight? In that stretch beyond ambition lies the territory of aspiration.

■

One of the great and bewildering challenges you face as a
student is figuring out how to aspire and doing so in a way that is
true to yourself and to your responsibilities. How do you go about
forming and internalizing aspirations?

✔ *Aspiration means using your studies as an avenue to
lasting honor and reward.* Give idealism a chance. Imagine good
qualities and achievements for which you want to be known and
the career that will facilitate those aspirations. Try to set your sights
on achieving something good for its own sake. This demands a certain amount of daring, and it calls for persistence, vision, and self-
discipline.

✔ *Aspiration means putting what you learn to good use.*
You can't aspire unless you know much, and you cannot know much
unless you read widely, study hard, and reflect at length about what
you have learned. Aspiration comes from knowledge of what others
have done, what they've come to consider valuable and good, and
how they've worked, often against great odds, to achieve what they
set out to do. To gain this knowledge, you must read of other people
in other times and other places, not just of those whose aspirations
were much like yours. You must try to learn of people substantially
different from you and of other endeavors substantially different from
your own. That way, you shape your dreams and form your aspirations from wide knowledge, not limited vision.

✔ *Developing your own aspirations requires you to study the aspirations of others.* This is another way of seeking counsel from those you consider trustworthy, prudent, and wise. Some of these people you may know, but others will be the authors of books you read, the explorers of the natural and physical world you live in, the figures of the history you learn, and the creators of the art you see and hear. Some say it is difficult to learn from the past. But you can still be guided by those in the past about whom you learn. Their guidance doesn't come to you directly as a set of instructions or commandments. Instead, you have to tease it out from what you learn and then give it your own meaning. That's one of the ways you convert inert information into active understanding.

✔ *Aspiration means always keeping in mind the legacy you'd like to leave behind.* We are inundated these days with news of those who are "stars," people whom we see and hear in the media and who entertain us. But while their celebrity may gain them present notice, true achievement wins the renown of posterity. Those who are renowned are people who have achieved something exceptional, often in obscurity, sometimes at the sacrifice of their well-being. They are remembered by later generations for their contributions to human welfare. Those who achieve something lasting usually do so because they understand better, through long study and reflection, how to create something that has never been made or seen before. They struggle to overcome daunting obstacles to knowledge, pushing against their repeated frustrations and failures to achieve their goals. To be sure, we recall many scoundrels. But it's the lives of people of great achievement—George Washington, Susan B. Anthony, and Martin Luther King, Jr.—that we should emulate in the hope that, in our own ways and circumstances, we can achieve as much as they did.

✔ *To decide what you wish to leave behind requires that you look inside yourself.* Authenticity—being true to your deepest and most worthy hopes—is the key to your aspirations. Although you may not be the sole or even best judge of what you're capable of achieving, you must take your life's bearings from the compass within you. That's where you will find direction, and from there you'll be able to steer yourself for the life you define. But you can do so only if you're honest about what you want and what you can achieve, and only if you bring to bear upon your search for a good life all the learning you have gained in all your years of study. If undertaken earnestly and well, your education should have provided you already with a storehouse of knowledge on which to draw as you try to live your life well and realize your aspirations and dreams.

Of course, other people are available, and should be sought, to give you advice about your abilities, your promise, and your future. But by the time you're in high school, and surely by the time you receive your diploma, your life has become your own. The mistakes you make are your responsibility, not your parents', teachers', or coaches', and each day someone you used to lean on will urge you to stand on your own feet, and to pick yourself up when you happen to fall.

This means that the achievements you begin to record by the time you're in high school are more creditable to you than to others. It's now your life, and it's largely your own determination and will that control it, not your background, environment, family, or upbringing. It now falls to you alone to design your life. And the best way to do that is to reach high and let yourself be guided by what you've learned. At the point where knowledge and aspiration intersect, many of the personal qualities you've brought to bear on your work as a student produce their most exciting results.

Yuan Greene didn't know what she wanted to do with her life. Adults were always asking her what she hoped to be when she grew up, but an answer always eluded her. Many of her high school friends had precise plans for themselves, but she thought that it was far too soon to make such long-term commitments. While everyone had suggestions and advice to give her, nobody could persuade her that she should begin to narrow her choices before she had even reached college.

She felt roughly the same way about her high school motto — "Honor your Heritage." Like the other students, she couldn't understand it. If honoring her heritage would lead to a satisfying life, Yuan was quite willing to obey the motto's injunction, but she couldn't figure out in what particular direction it pointed. She was pretty sure it didn't mean that she should become an embezzler like her grandfather, who, despite his skills, had been found out and had gone to jail for his crimes. But what, then? Did her heritage have something to do with trying to make more money than her parents?

Anyway, how could she know what her heritage was? The child of Chinese parents who had been Buddhists, she had been adopted as an infant by a Jewish father and a Catholic mother born in Mexico. And when she tried to interpret that well-known term, "the American heritage," she concluded that it was as much a heritage of slavery and degradation of the environment as a glorious one of free speech and general economic well-being.

Furthermore, she'd already concluded that in the United States you could do pretty much as you wanted and forget about your heritage. Yuan feared that if she tried to honor her heritage she'd go crazy in the process; and like most of her classmates, she rolled her eyes whenever the school's principal once again urged the students to think about it.

But as her classmates had to concede, the phrase—probably because it was repeated so often—worked its way into their consciousness. Wanted or not, it was always there, like a loyal dog. The students wrote humorous verses about it and composed football cheers from its words. It cropped up in every school publication.

Yuan's schoolmates began to think of the motto as something like the weather: it was there, and there wasn't much you could do about it.

Then Yuan forgot it. When she went off to college, she put that motto, and all the other baggage she'd acquired at school, behind her. No more study halls, no more required class attendance, no more lectures from the principal, and no more honoring her heritage. Freedom at last!

Yet independence, she soon found out, only intensified the responsibility she had to assume for herself. And, each day, the future—that future of adult work and the choice of profession—came closer. As freshman year turned into sophomore and then junior years, her parents stepped up their nagging questions about what she was going to do, and she noticed that more and more of her friends were attending career fairs and beginning to plan for work after graduation. But when she asked them why they were doing this, they answered only that they were expected to do so—hardly, to her mind, a compelling reason. Not that she had any idea of what she wanted to do, either; she was equally confused about her future. She knew that she had to face that future. But she also knew that she didn't want to take the first job that came along. What was she to do?

Out of nowhere one day, that old school motto came into Yuan's mind. Oh no, she thought, not that. What did it mean? Honor: how was she to do that? Perhaps, it began to dawn on her, her heritage was one of good fortune—a comfortable childhood, the best education, life in an open society. So honoring it might mean using that good fortune for the benefit of others. It had to mean more than entering a sales program or using her computer programming skills for an advertising agency.

One day, after a seminar in history, it came to her in a flash. "Here I am," she thought to herself, "a Chinese-American raised by a Jew and a Catholic who is lucky enough to be attending this great university. Not only that, I have this opportunity without being threatened by the kind of ignorant discrimination someone with my

What To Do: Adapt!

Because you never know what you are going to make of what you learn, learning always involves a risk of some sort. When you study and gain new knowledge, you often have to change your mind, adjust your thinking, or accept the possibility of alternative ways of looking at the world. If you stop daring to learn, you stop growing.

✔ *Open yourself to new knowledge.* A closed mind cannot learn, nor can it understand. Yet an open mind doesn't require you to give up what you know or believe. It only means that you're prepared to consider new ideas. As Yogi Berra urged us, "When you come to a crossroad, take it."

✔ *Try out new knowledge.* Play with it. Make intellectual risk a working method of study. Don't dismiss facts or ideas that may trouble you at first. Keep them with you. Reflect on them. See whether they fit with what you already know. Retain what you must, but change your mind if you have to.

✔ *Test your convictions by considering different or opposing ones.* That is probably the best way to strengthen your own beliefs. And the best reason to change them if you must is that you have concluded that other ideas have greater validity.

✔ *Accept the discipline of fact.* Sometimes that discipline is harsh and discomforting. It forces you to risk accepting what is so because it's so. But you must be prepared to accept what is known and proven to be true, even at the cost of surrendering old beliefs.

complex background—and female to boot—would suffer in most other countries. Perhaps I should try to learn how that happened and try to explain it to others. Maybe that's what it means to honor *my* heritage."

That thought stayed with her until one day she happened to talk with a recruiter for the federal civil service, who suggested that she might look into immigration and naturalization work. That did it. Soon after graduation, she began helping immigrants become citizens, and later she decided to enter a graduate program in ethnic studies so that she could teach others about the complexities of ethnicity. That old high school motto had made sense after all, she informed her old friends when she returned for their tenth reunion. "I finally know what it means."

7

· · · · · · · · · · · · · · · · · · · ·

Imagination

Our imaginations are in danger of withering away. Because television, films, and computers have made images so graphic and immediate, we no longer have to think of what might be; instead, we're shown how it is. If a character in a movie is to be decapitated, the screen shows the guillotine's blade descend, then the steel biting into the victim's neck, and finally his severed head tumbling into a basket, as a gush of ketchup douses the executioner's robe. In earlier days of the cinema, the same effect was achieved by showing the blade descend, then cutting to a shot of the bystanders' faces, as a dull thump is heard on the soundtrack. Whether this art of allusion was practiced subtly or crudely, viewers were expected to invent their own picture of the actual beheading.

So it has to be with your own imagination: you have to create poetry, humor, beauty, and understanding out of all sorts of otherwise simple facts, words, and pictures. And you can't depend on anyone else for imagination. It is the most private and interior of human faculties. That's why somebody else explaining a poem's allusions—or, worse, explaining a joke—makes the effect pointless. If you don't get the joke, explaining it only destroys it. As with comedy, so with poems: the best

English teacher in the world is going to have a hard time attracting you to poetry unless you develop the capacity to "get it" for yourself. Imagination is like a key: it unlocks the door to knowledge.

Consider, for example, Wallace Stevens's poem "The Emperor of Ice Cream." Like so many modern poems, its images are indirect; he uses words as an Impressionist painter uses brush strokes—

Using Your Imagination

Some people think that imagination works with sudden surprise, like a lightning flash from a clear blue sky. Yet it can be summoned and applied just like other human qualities. What you have to do to summon it is to know that it's there and then to harness it.

If you can get control of your imagination and apply it directly to some chosen problem, you may be startled by what happens. Think of Newton's laws of gravity or the Constitution of the United States. Each was the result of applied study—of mathematics in one case, of history and law in the other—and then of imagining what was not yet but might be.

So what can you do to exercise and use your imagination?

Free yourself from your inner censor. No one can know what you are thinking in the privacy of your own mind, so no one can laugh at you, attack you, or hate you on account of it. So let your imagination roam free. Think of ways, even silly ways, to understand what you're studying or to give your new knowledge meaning.

Put what you're learning together in new, even unlikely, combinations. This is the key to creativity, a route to understanding. New combinations can help you understand more easily what you're studying, or to glimpse it in a new light. Sometimes, they can yield an idea or a creation that has never existed before. All great poetry is like that, and much science, too.

Make the abstract concrete. This may not seem to have anything to do with your imagination, but it does. You have to imagine how much of what you are learning might apply to your life. Sometimes you learn by figuring out problems that are naturally concrete—using geometry, say, to figure out the shortest route from your home to a friend's. In other subjects, however, you have to work hard to create concrete applications for what you're learning. Because it helps you learn, it's worth the effort.

Discipline your imagination. A contradiction? Not really. If your imagination wanders aimlessly, it's not likely to hit upon anything of use or significance. But if you put some fencing around it, you're likely to get results. What form can that "fencing" take? Questions, for one thing; specific assignments—especially self-imposed ones—for another. Keep asking yourself what everything means. Press yourself to figure out how what you're learning might apply to your own life and interests. That's how knowledge "sticks."

to imply and suggest, but not to state or declare. Stevens's meaning is purposefully unclear, as if he were saying to us, "Bring what you want to the poem, and give it some meaning yourself, but don't rely on me to guide you." That makes the poem "difficult," which is probably what you'll think when you first read it. But its lack of clarity is also what makes the poem so potent. It's like a piece of wet clay, which you can shape into many things. Try being a sculptor with the poem.

> Call the roller of big cigars,
> The muscular one, and bid him whip

> In kitchen cups the concupiscent curds.
> Let the wenches dawdle in such dress
> As they are used to wear, and let the boys
> Bring flowers in last month's newspapers.
> Let be be finale of seem.
> The only emperor is the emperor of ice cream.
>
> Take from the dresser of deal,
> Lacking the three glass knobs, that sheet
> On which she embroidered fantails once
> And spread it so as to cover her face.
> If her horny feet protrude, they come
> To show how cold she is, and dumb.
> Let the lamp affix its beam.
> The only emperor is the emperor of ice cream.

It shouldn't be surprising if you're puzzled. "The Emperor of Ice Cream" is complex, and it may be the kind of poem you've never read before. So you might begin by asking yourself what impressions each of the two stanzas makes on you. Some interpreters have thought the first stanza suggests life and that the second is about death. Similarly, there's a kind of holiday mood in the first, while the second, if you take it to be about an event, seems to introduce a funeral, with everyone's attention focused on the corpse. So you might ask yourself what kind of empire this emperor rules over.

So far, you might concede, this makes sense, but beyond this point no one is likely to agree, because the poem's effects will touch each reader's mind differently and prompt a unique interpretation in each. The poem isn't a journey that all must travel together from A to B but a labyrinth in which each of us gets lost differently. The fascination and pleasure of the poem lie in this complexity.

An example of extended allusion like Stevens's poem is one of the greatest challenges language can offer to the imagination. If a poem has no immediate meaning for you, you must, to give it meaning—not, as others might say, to "figure out" its meaning—read and reread it, perhaps use a dictionary or an encyclopedia, even read what others may have said about it. But above all, you have to try to picture the poem's scenes and events in the secret theater of your imagination. You have to connect the words and images of the poem just as you have to link the points in a connect-the-dots puzzle in order to give them significance. And then what the scenes and events in the poem come to mean for you is what, in the end, they actually mean. Imagination has made the poem your own.

You may think that imagination is relevant only to the arts, but it is also important in such "hard" fields as the sciences. A scientific discovery rarely presents itself to a scientist as the final step in a long chain of experiments that produce inevitably and logically some new outcome. Instead, scientists have to apply their imaginations— which are schooled and disciplined, of course, by long study and experience—to solve previously insoluble problems.

In fact, because scientists can't resolve some questions about reality, they often agree that sharply different, sometimes contradictory, explanations may be equally satisfactory ways of understanding certain phenomena. That's necessary because much of what becomes known through experimentation cannot be seen by the human eye and because no single theory seems to make sense of what becomes known.

For instance, it's not clear whether light is made up of waves or particles. The way scientists deal with this uncertainty is to imagine light as being made of both, even though they can see neither. In this way they can ask questions that wouldn't come to their minds if they gave up thinking of light altogether because they couldn't identify or measure its constituent parts.

It's similar with Stevens's poem. He wrote it, and presumably it had a certain meaning for him. But we don't know what that meaning was, even though the poem exists on paper to solicit our speculation. Either we ignore it or, in order to understand it as best we can, we imagine, through careful analysis, what it might mean.

That way, it means what we interpret it to mean through knowledge and imagination.

■

The imagination that contributes even to science is arguably the most natural and universal human quality. It is among the earliest and most enjoyable traits we possess. Small children delight in games of "let's pretend," which send them on endless flights of fancy. A chair can be an airplane, a paper box a magic carpet, in a make-believe world better than anything that the children see around them. And children don't really need props. They can say "Let's pretend we have a magic carpet," and they're off into the realm of their fancies. Reality isn't exciting enough for their games. Perhaps that's why they like fairy tales and stories of monsters, ogres, and witches.

But as you grow older, your teachers place less emphasis on your imagination and more on empirical facts and known phenomena. The adult world of reality begins to beckon, and your imagination begins to wither, or it's channeled into the private pleasures of reading science fiction or medieval fantasy. As the years go by, you may doubt whether you still possess the ability to create a world of make-believe for yourself, and yet this ability is essential to your fulfillment as a student. Although your teachers will sometimes stimulate you to use your imagination, this play of the mind is usually left to you to engage in on your own. It's something you must activate for yourself.

Why is imagination so important to you?

✔ *Imagination allows you to see yourself as a student.* You may see yourself performing as a dancer or an athlete or socializing as a popular person. But if you turn your imagination in another direction, you can also see yourself studying, learning, and finding satisfaction in what you come to know. Envisioning yourself learning often plays a key role in helping you to learn effectively. It's worth trying to summon up that image.

✔ *Imagination makes creative and active what is otherwise inert and passive.* Like the dead frog you have to dissect in biology class, much of what you're offered in the classroom lacks a certain vitality. That quality you have to supply. Think of "The Emperor of Ice Cream." The poet is little help to you in understanding his work. But the pleasure of the poem lies in giving his words your own discovered meaning and thereby understanding them. Likewise, recognizing participles and gerunds in English grammar—haven't you been asked to distinguish between the two and failed to remember the difference?—can appear as dry as the Gobi Desert until, working with the verb "to laugh," you explain to yourself why laughing gas and laughing clowns differ grammatically—and dramatically.

Imagination gives what you're learning the significance that it otherwise may not possess. Imagine yourself a preeminent brain surgeon. Rock stars and world leaders come to you when they need someone to check under their hoods, and other doctors brandish scalpels at twenty paces for the privilege of assisting you in your operating theater. Your fees bankrupt billionaires, and you have a waiting list for your talents that will pay for your five grandchildren's college education and still keep you in comfortable retirement. What's more, you're renowned for developing never-before-attempted procedures that have revolutionized brain surgery forever. Where did this daydream begin? In high school biology class, just before you cut open your first dead frog. Of what use is the fantasy? It fuels you to work hard to gain the knowledge necessary to achieve what you dream about.

✔ *Although imagination is naturally unruly, it can be—and for a student must be—brought under some discipline.* Going from a dead frog in formaldehyde to a productive life of good medical deeds and comfortable wealth is a nice fancy, but usually your imagination is neither so orderly nor so practical. So you've got to learn to put it to work on specific tasks and not let it wander off each time on its own. The best way to do that is to give the hard work you're engaged in some personal meaning, especially if the work is required and not of your own choosing. Differential calculus? Surely no need for that since I'm going to be an art historian, you may say. But because the subject has to do with the measurement of rates of change when component variables change, perhaps you can conceptualize a calculus of developments in medieval architecture as various aspects of medieval society themselves changed. There's no telling what imagination can do when you choose to give something a meaning it didn't have before.

✔   *Imagination, like falling in love, can make the ordinary magical.* Turning a page in a book that grips your mind or completing a difficult laboratory experiment can be as exciting and as full of expectation as the touch of a lover's hand. Of course, it may be hard to invest differential calculus with quite the same excitement or significance. And if you do, the world may think you're slightly crazy, just as it often regards people who are, as it's sometimes put, "madly in love." But what's at stake is your ability to learn. So your own private imagination, like enthusiasm and curiosity, ought to be an accomplice to everything you do to study and learn.

✔   *Imagination generates humor, interest, and pleasure when you study and learn.* It does so by creating pictures in your mind, many of them so far from reality as to be ridiculous. And if those images are so far-fetched as to make you laugh, why should you care as long as they bring you illumination and the energy to work harder? In fact, a principal path to happiness is an industrious imagination. It's because of imagination, according to Samuel Johnson, that a man may be as happy in the arms of a chambermaid as in those of a duchess—or, as we'd update the adage, that a woman may be as happy in the arms of a gardener as in those of a duke. Thanks to your imagination, you'll find that you can be as happy in your calculus class as you can be eating ice cream with the emperor.

No one can prescribe what you should imagine, and, as you've noticed, even you can't always discipline your imagination: it goes in directions that sometimes leave you, its ostensible master, mystified. It is private, personal, and unique. It is the playground in your head. You can't share much of it with anyone else, unless you know and trust that person. That's why your imagination is so powerful an implement in your struggle to study and learn: it's yours alone, and any way you can find to employ it in that service is bound to be helpful.

In some respects, too, imagination is the most powerful aid to learning and creating knowledge that you possess. It may help if you think of a great artist like Michelangelo chipping away at a block of marble to reveal, as he put it, the statue hiding inside. Imagination is the means by which you reveal to yourself the concealed treasures that already lie within you.

✎

Mary Lombardi was the kind of student who makes a simple problem much more difficult and complex than it really is.

In her second year of college, her academic record was nothing to boast about. But her record, mediocre as it was, was not her greatest worry. For a year she had wrestled with choosing a major, something every college sophomore is expected to do. She had flirted with psychology, business administration, Spanish, biology, and history. Yet her interest in all these subjects was minimal, and her grades were no better or worse in one than in another.

Then she happened on an English course with a charismatic professor, and, she thought, her choice was assured. In any case, she had always claimed that she loved literature. So because reading works of literature made up a significant component of an undergraduate major in English, she decided to major in the subject.

Unfortunately, though she found literature appealing, she

hated to read. It soon dawned on her that a major in English required great quantities of what she detested to do. And while her friends were quick to point out the inconsistency between loving literature and hating to read, labeling the dilemma that way didn't help her resolve it. What was she to do?

Her hatred of reading was so intense that she couldn't imagine herself ever liking to read, as others did. And so she'd never tried hard to read or to figure out what her favorite kinds of books might be. Because she couldn't imagine herself as a reader, there seemed little point in struggling to imagine what she might read. And it would have been a struggle in any case, for she was characteristically unimaginative.

Fortunately, her academic adviser was no stranger to these kinds of problems. He knew that no one is born with a taste for reading; like most other tastes, it must first be imagined and then acquired. To get Mary to read with ease and pleasure, he had to find some way to get her to envision herself reading. He met with her at the end of her sophomore year. What, he asked her, would she most like to read if only she didn't hate reading. "I really don't know," she answered. "That's no help," he said. "If you're going to major in English, you've got to read. So what's your choice? What's the topic you dislike the least?" She had never considered such a question. "Well," she said, "my mother's a private investigator, and I've always loved to hear stories of her work. So maybe I'd like mysteries."

Unknown to Mary, her clever adviser had found the key to her problem. "Okay," he said. "Imagine yourself reading crime novels. What kind would you prefer?" "Actually, none," she said, "because then I'd have to read." "This isn't getting us anywhere," snapped her adviser. So Mary acknowledged that if she couldn't escape reading, she might have an inclination toward tales of women detectives.

Before she knew it, her adviser guided her to the library armed with a list of crime novels with female protagonists. With his encouragement, Mary heroically forced herself to read at least one work of crime fiction a week. It wasn't easy going; she had to fight hard against her powerful aversion. Within a week, she was back in her adviser's office, telling him that she couldn't get into the books at all. She was ready to give up. But he suggested that she should imagine that the female sleuths were her mother; doing so might bring the characters to life for her.

So Mary tried again and found her mother playing the most unlikely roles, from Hollywood starlet to proper elderly English spinster in a quiet country village. Apart from the amusement she and her parent got when Mary told her of her make-believe disguises, Mary began to find herself reading with interest, pleasure, and speed. She began even to compare one author with another, one approach to crime novels with others, on her own. And when she returned to campus in the fall, she found that, though still not easy, reading was no longer an ordeal. She even got a B in her Shakespeare course.

Later in life when she had trouble motivating herself to read —her youthful distaste for it never fully left her—she would call up the image of all those summer hours spent trying to get over her antipathy for books. And she would find that simply thinking of herself sitting with a book in her hand, reading about women detectives, got her back into a frame of mind so that she could read without too much pain.

What To Do: Apply What You Learn!

Application makes what you learn stick in your mind. But applying knowledge is easier said than done. For while some subjects you learn, such as mathematics, have clear applicability, others, like literature, don't. So you have to learn to think of applicability in different ways.

✔ *Think of the application of knowledge not as a way to do something but as a way to think.* Math is useful in finance, but it has a more important utility: learning it can give you the ability to think deeply and well. Some say that literature has no practical use—as if understanding life better and being able to write accurately and speak articulately have no value! They're wrong.

✔ *Try to apply everything you learn to something that is relevant to you.* After you have read a novel, think of people you know who are similar to some of its characters and try to understand them better. After you have run a physics problem, find an appliance that illustrates the physics principle you've just explored.

✔ *Think of yourself in a context.* Imagine yourself as a character in a play or as a leading figure in history. Then review that character's situation and imagine making momentous choices the way the person whose part you're assuming might have to make them.

8

Self-Discipline

The word *discipline* conjures up all kinds of negative images: your parents sending you to your room for misbehaving, teachers making you stay after school for not turning in your homework, or a coach benching you for missing practice—all of them unpleasant consequences by which your freedom is constrained. So you may think of discipline as an unwarranted limitation on your thought, conduct, and expression, as well as a denial of your welfare and natural self. And it's true that a Hitler or a Stalin will impose discipline that's illegitimate, unjust, and contrary to humane values.

But in a disorderly world, external discipline is essential. Discipline is necessary both for the sake of the young and for controlling people, like criminals, who cause harm to others. Also, external rules of conduct and systems of rewards and punishments are the universal means of helping you develop the internal, ordered ways that are essential for your own good and that of society as a whole.

So at some stage, your parents and teachers assume that they've done what they can through the imposition of external guidance. They step back and turn over to you the responsibility for conducting yourself appropriately. They hope that discipline will now be self-imposed, that you've graduated from discipline to self-discipline, that you've become your own best boss.

Self-discipline doesn't mean forcing yourself to write "I won't misplace a comma again" a hundred times on the blackboard

Going for the Gold

Self-discipline is hard to achieve if you have no goals. Tests of self, the order you impose on your life as a student, are made much more tolerable and rewarding if they're hooked to some aspiration. If, like Olympic athletes, you "go for the gold"—whatever that level of success may mean for you—then you ought to be able to gain from your struggle with the many frustrations and disappointments of hard, disciplined study deep satisfaction and contentment. But how can you do so?

Keep clearly in mind why you're undergoing the self-imposed "punishments" of self-discipline. Your aspiration—the reason for your struggle to learn—is what justifies the torments of self-discipline. When the going is really tough, it's especially important to remind yourself of what you are trying to achieve. Fortify yourself with thoughts of your goal, and study to achieve it.

Remember that your own high aspirations free you from others' expectations. This is internalized freedom, the result of internalized order. As long as your purpose is worthy and your means of seeking it reasonable and ethical, no one will keep you from steering your own course. If you know where you want to go and learn all there is to get there, no one is likely to deter you.

Adjust for need, not for fashion. The life of a student offers all sorts of distractions and seductions—easy courses, your concern for popularity, extracurricular activities. Don't let them come between you and your studies. Revise your goals or your program for achieving them only for the strongest reasons—health, perhaps, or the recognition that you've chosen a goal unsuited to your talents. But don't give them up if you haven't first reevaluated your aspirations and goals.

for a mistake in punctuation. Nor do we expect you to strike yourself over the hand with a heavy ruler for talking in class, as every schoolteacher depicted in nineteenth-century British novels appears to do. We have something far milder—yet far more demanding—in mind: that you determine the order, methods, and conduct required to help yourself as a student. Once you're enrolled in your classes, once homework and required lab experiments are handed out, and once exams are scheduled, you are on your own. Only you can go to class, read your assignments, or take your exams. You've got to find a way to do so under your own steam.

You're probably thinking, "That's what they've been telling me all my life. What else is new? I know that." But you may not have realized how directly self-discipline affects your welfare as a student and how difficult it is to develop and maintain.

Developing the quality of self-discipline can be a solitary task. While others can tell whether you possess self-discipline and can provide you with good examples of it by what they do, they can't do much directly to help you develop the trait. You alone must become used to long hours of study and must develop the qualities you'll need to master a subject. Self-discipline also calls for some kinds of behavior that, at least at first, you'll find unappealing—putting off socializing with your friends, for example, and planning ahead for a paper or a final exam.

Yet for all the frustrations it may bring you, self-discipline is a highly positive force during your years as a student—and through-out your life. It makes you the sole architect of your own life. It helps you gain the self-reliance that enables you to design your own char-acter and increase your own knowledge through study and reflec-tion. It manifests the personal efforts you've undertaken to impose order on the natural confusions of life, efforts for which no one else can take credit. Rather than being a curb or a restriction on you, self-discipline is a dimension of personal freedom.

What do we mean by self-discipline? It's the order you im-pose on yourself out of full understanding of what is best for you. Self-discipline is structured industry, some kind of plan or method by which you direct your efforts and schedule your time. It's study and activity tied to your aspirations and pursued with perseverance and method. For everyone, that plan will differ; but for everyone that plan is essential.

Not that the plan needs to be written down or followed slavishly. But to learn and study most effectively, you need to have a clear idea of what you're trying to achieve, some program to achieve it, and enough self-knowledge to understand how to implement it. You may study best in the afternoon. Perhaps you can tackle only two subjects a day. Maybe you're the kind of person who can read attentively for three hours straight or work in a lab all morning. But whatever your tastes and rhythms are, you have to figure out how to use them to your best advantage and to do so in some kind of ordered way. Then hard work will become more satisfying, and the time you spend learning will be more productive.

But developing self-discipline doesn't mean focusing exclu-sively on yourself. It doesn't mean that you have to exclude other people from your life. It doesn't justify extreme forms of selfish be-havior. (You can't, after all, rob a bank simply because the loot would solve your financial problems.) Nor does self-discipline justify over-

looking the interests, feelings, and needs of others, for you have social, ethical, and legal responsibilities.

Self-discipline does mean, however, that you have to look to
yourself for the order that you're trying to create. It means building
an internal structure to your life out of the knowledge you accumulate about the world. Once you have done that, all sorts of benefits
accrue. Remembering what you learn is made easier, for example, by
reviewing what you know—by making use of the structure of knowledge you have created within yourself. Also, deciding what you'll try
to achieve grows out of the knowledge of yourself and of the world
that you gain through disciplined study.

These are no easy tasks. Chaos and incoherence—the absence of order and discipline—reign everywhere. Read the daily
newspaper headlines and monitor the passage of your thoughts and
the changes in your emotions. Once you do so, you'll have a fuller
appreciation of why so many great myths about the creation of the
world start off by describing the imposition of order on chaos. Those
myths endure because we have an innate sense that harmony must
replace discord and that confusion must yield to structure if self and
society are to exist.

The theme of order through self-discipline appears again
and again in works of literature. You're probably familiar with the
themes of J. D. Salinger's modern classic *The Catcher in the Rye,*
usually thought of as a novel about individuality and alienation. Yet
it's also about order and disorder. The book's appealing protagonist,
Holden Caulfield, gets into no end of difficulties because his disorderly
mind, tongue, and emotions dart repeatedly and randomly from one
subject to another. His story illustrates the fact, among other things,
that the creation of structure within your mind and order in your
emotions is a difficult and often painful process. Like Holden—who
doesn't do a good job of it—you have to bring order to your inner
and outer life on your own. The world may not be orderly, but you
must try to be so.

How is it best to think about the quality of self-discipline?

✔ *Self-discipline means considering your own welfare as a student.* This requires you to resist the lure of those activities that don't contribute to your accumulation of knowledge, and it demands that you keep the necessary growth of your understanding uppermost in your mind. When you're learning, you're doing so only for yourself. When you fail to learn, you're squandering an opportunity that benefits nobody but yourself.

✔ *Self-discipline means setting high standards for yourself.* That's part of seeing to your own welfare. It's also one way to free yourself from standards which are annoying simply because others apply them. If you can internalize your own standards and measure your progress toward knowledge and understanding against them, you'll attain a new kind of freedom. You'll be your toughest judge. In adopting high standards, you can adopt those set by your teachers—if those standards are high enough. Better yet, consider setting higher ones, even ones that are slightly beyond you. The purpose is not to court failure but to hold out the possibility of learning more than you thought possible.

✔ *Your self-discipline must have direction.* You need to tie the inner order you're working to create to something you wish to achieve, and you need to have some positive reason for trying to achieve it. This may mean making hard choices among competing interests and desires. Unless you have as many natural gifts as a Leonardo da Vinci or a Thomas Jefferson, it does little good for you to order your life around ten different, beloved interests without emphasizing a few of them and allowing some of the others to take second place. Instead, you should establish your priorities and work toward achieving them.

✔ *Self-discipline means postponing immediate gratification for later, and greater, benefits.* This may be the most difficult dimension of self-discipline. It brings to mind caricatures of self-denial —people who fear, in the American writer H. L. Mencken's memorable phrase, "that somewhere someone may be happy." Yet self-discipline does, of course, require some self-denial, some putting off of what would give you pleasure now in the interest of gains that will bring you immeasurably greater benefits later on.

It's hard to tell your friends that you're not going somewhere with them because you have to study. It's hard to tell your parents that you're not going to return home for the holidays because staying on campus to work on your upcoming term papers will increase your chances of admission to graduate school. Nor are we recommending that you take such actions as a matter of course; after all, you can learn from friends and family, too. But occasionally making those tough choices may lead to more knowledge. And that's usually in your best interest.

Though lonely and demanding, self-discipline, when achieved, is exhilarating. You have to achieve what you seek by yourself; and to achieve it you must often try and try again, through exhausting practice and repetition. Yet once you finish what's required —after you read and reread your assignments, run and run again those experiments—the payoff is enduring. "At last!" you'll shout. "At last I understand why the colonists declared their independence!" "At last I understand what Shakespeare's characters are saying to each other!" "So that's the significance of the second law of thermodynamics!" And, to add particular pleasure to such achievements, you've gained what you sought through your own devices; you've set your sights on learning something, and you have done so on your own. There are few greater satisfactions than imposing this kind of order upon yourself and attaining new knowledge as a result.

Jordan Jones played on his high school's football team. He had a lively sense of fun, hung out with other students, and looked forward to vacations. The school's many organizations only mildly interested him, except for the African-American Students' Club, where he had many close friends. His grade reports were usually a mixture of B's with an occasional C or an A, showing that he had few major academic weaknesses but also few major strengths.

When those unanticipated midwinter holidays known as snow days occurred, most of Jordan's friends spent the day enjoying themselves indoors and out. Jordan would join them for an hour or two and play as hard as any of them. But then he'd go home to study, even though they'd plead with him to stay and then scoff at his sudden seriousness. He saw these unexpected free days not simply as a chance to relax but as an opportunity to catch up with an assignment or prepare for a test. Although Jordan's classmates knew him to be determined to do as well as he could, "School's for fun," they'd argue. "If school's just for fun," he'd answer, "then why do teachers give tests and make us write papers? They're no fun. School's not for fun; it's for getting ahead."

"You're crazy," some of his friends would taunt. "Why are you so serious about school?" "I'm just trying to do the best I can," he'd respond, hoping that he didn't sound ridiculous. Usually, he didn't seem so: in the eyes of most of his friends, that straightforward determination was Jordan's great strength. Not a brilliant student, he nevertheless kept his eye firmly on what he'd come to expect of himself without becoming self-absorbed. He met his obligations to the football team. He went out on weekends. But he never neglected his coursework, even if it caused him to miss out on something he wanted to do.

And he hated missing good times with his friends. He feared that his absence from some activities would make him less popular; and as much as anyone else he enjoyed taking it easy and not working hard. Yet he was determined to make the most of school and to compile as good a record for college admissions as possible. The only way to do that, he reasoned, was to keep working hard in his courses, to do all his homework, to write his required papers early so that he could revise them, and to study hard for exams. And if doing so meant putting aside some other activities he'd also like to pursue— well, he'd just have to put them aside. Jordan's friends marveled at how impossible it was to knock him off course.

Characteristically, when the time came to apply to college, Jordan had carefully assessed his chances for admission. He succeeded in getting into the three colleges to which he'd applied and chose what his teachers agreed was the best one for him. And not surprisingly, he followed the same determined course in college as he had in school. But that's part of another story.

What To Do: Share Your Knowledge!

Learning is solitary; it can "take" as knowledge only inside your own mind. And it is often lonely; most of the time you have to study and learn by yourself. But learning is always an exchange between you and someone else—your teachers, the authors of what you read and the creators of what you examine, or your fellow students—that is, people who help you learn.

✔ *Learn with others.* Try studying with a group. Or review your notes and prepare for examinations with your fellow students. Ask them questions; let them test you. It will never do harm to exchange ideas about how to approach a problem or examine a text.

✔ *Teach others.* Help your fellow students learn what they, too, are struggling to learn, what they don't know or understand. By helping others, you'll learn what every teacher knows: that nothing makes something stick in the mind more securely than having to explain it to someone else.

✔ *Allow others to teach you.* Ask them to assist you in learning what you're studying. Find out how they came to understand something difficult. Learn their "tricks." Finding out how others learn is a major part of your own learning.

9

. . . .

Civility

Civility is a term that has gone out of fashion, and it now often carries negative connotations. That's in part because many people who wish to make the term useful again have a particular meaning for it—sometimes coercive, often one-dimensional. They see civility only as an aspect of order. In fact, it's an aspect of responsibility—toward others. When *civility* is restored to its full meaning, which summarizes the virtues needed in a member of a community, its bad reputation melts away, and it regains its place as a useful term. For whether we think that the world has become less civil or more so, examples of civility, as well as incivility, abound in our lives. If you identify them as such, you can see that you are engaged in acts of civility all the time when you learn. You can also see that the quality of civility has a direct bearing upon your endeavors as a student.

When you listen without interruption to an argument that you consider ridiculous, then criticize that argument without raising your voice or attacking the speaker's motives or intelligence, you are exhibiting civility. When, after a fellow student draws conclusions from a set of philosophical principles that you consider foolish, you call him an idiot, you're being uncivil. When you help clean up the lab so that the next class can use it without impediment, you're being civil. When you leave the mess from your experiments for the next class to deal with, you're not.

Civility is a dual quality. When you are civil, you acknowledge people's right to speak and act in ways that are not injurious to

Competition

For some students, competition against others is a spur to achievement. For others, it's paralyzing pressure. But even if you shun competition or don't think you do well when competing, you're always engaged, and ought to be engaged, in one kind of competition—competition with yourself.

You may believe that surpassing yourself requires competition with others—a desire to get better grades than they do, to defeat an opposing team in debate, or to attend a more prestigious college. In fact, you may need that competition to do well. Or you may find that the satisfaction of simply doing better than you did before—improving your grades, mastering a subject that defeated you earlier, or just coming to understand something that fills you with wonder—is enough to spur you on. Yet whatever kind of competition works best for you will always demand hard work. And if simple, applied industry is difficult for you to achieve, then perhaps the spur of competition, against either yourself or others, is what you need.

Competition is often criticized as alien to an ideal society. We hear it said that competition should be avoided so as to protect the more tender souls among us. Some argue that our society is already too competitive, adversarial, dog-eat-dog. And surely there's some truth to that.

Nevertheless, an urge to compete is built into many people, and it has often served as a motive for human achievement. The ancients recognized it—in their Olympic games, for example—as one source among many of honor and perfection. Prizes, such as the Nobel, are awarded in secret competition to people who are recognized as having gone beyond others in their contributions to knowledge and human betterment. And in our own society the competition for elective office, while often sordid, still represents the most legitimate procedure and central feature of a democratic society.

So if competition works well for you in your studies, you ought to put it to good use—not, surely, to the point of trampling on the sensibilities of others, but in such ways that it may spur you to learn as much as you can.

you or anyone else (whatever you may think of what they're saying or doing). You accept your active responsibilities toward them, and, trusting them, you assume their responsibilities toward you. Civility has to do with both your bearing and your acts—but not with your beliefs or feelings. In an important sense, civility is the other side of free speech: you listen to and tolerate what other people, like yourself, are free to say and do, and you restrain yourself from uttering hurtful words or committing hurtful acts. Civility is thus the side of the coin with "self-control" written on it, the other side carrying the legend "self-expression." You can't have a one-sided coin.

Civility is critical to your life as a student because it's the foundation of the respectful, generous, and quiet atmosphere of the classrooms, laboratories, and libraries in which you learn. It's also an essential quality of the open society in which you're fortunate enough to live. It is, so to speak, the basic "rule of the game" of ordered conduct and discussion, the principle by which you are expected to govern yourself in relation to others. And because it creates an aspect of outward order and calm when you may feel agitated and angry, civility usually moderates the way in which you express your grievances with others. It allows debate to take the place of violence.

The quality of civility is consequently more than courtesy, consideration, or respect—although it implies all these qualities. It governs the procedures and norms by which civilized society operates. Civility is the recognition of the right of others to think what they think, believe what they believe, and act as they choose to act as long as their thoughts, beliefs, and behavior don't pose a threat of harm to anyone else. This doesn't mean that civility requires you to agree with others or to refrain from criticizing them. Nor does it mean that others can't voice their differences with you or criticize what you do. Civility doesn't protect you against others' thinking you a fool. Such risk is unavoidable in open societies, where the latitude of permissible speech and conduct is wide. But by the same token, others aren't protected against your expression of disagreement with them. Civility levels the playing field. It puts everyone on the same footing of rights and responsibilities.

You have only to look around you to see the consequences of incivility. Nations are torn apart by sectarian and religious strife because people don't allow others with different views and beliefs to live in their midst. Arguments, instead of being countenanced as part of the ordinary search for understanding, are often seen as battles for power—struggles to annihilate those who disagree, those who have particular ethnic origins, or those who subscribe to specific beliefs or views. These attitudes infect schools and colleges as well as the councils of government in those countries and threaten the welfare of students. In those nations, students are not free, as you are, to express themselves without fear of reprisal, even death. There, Thomas Jefferson's vision that "error of opinion may be tolerated where reason is left free to combat it" is unknown. There, incivility has dominion.

Clearly, civility is not an easy quality to develop, even in an open society such as ours. Instances of incivility—of thoughtless expression, disturbing conduct, and unneighborly acts—occur every day. And, in truth, don't you often want to strangle a classmate or a neighbor, to ridicule someone publicly for his views, or to embarrass someone for her attitudes? Those are normal feelings.

The trouble with acting upon them, however, is that any actions you take to prevent others from expressing their views reduce and probably close off the chance that you'll learn from them, because you haven't kept your mind open. Such acts also sharply increase the chances that others will act similarly toward you and not learn from what you have to say. In recognizing and acting upon a responsibility toward other students, in effect you serve your own interests, and you hope that others will act with the same calm, dignity, and respect for your rights of self-expression.

■

Civility, then, is basic to the advance of knowledge and the search for understanding and truth. Yet the development of civility is particularly difficult because it requires you to distinguish ideas and arguments from the character of the person who holds them. It asks you to separate in your mind the speaker from what's spoken, the author from what's written, the artist from what's painted—and to assess the validity or beauty of the creation free of evaluation of the character or conduct of the person who created it.

Surely one of the challenges of study is to strengthen and refine the quality of your discernment and judgment to distinguish the good from the bad. You also have to rise to the challenge of assessing quality, genuineness, and validity wherever it may arise and for whatever motive. That requires you to accept the possibility that people you don't like or with whom you normally disagree may speak or discover truth and contribute to your own understanding. You also have to allow those people to express themselves freely as long as they don't threaten you in doing so.

Facts, knowledge, points of view, and theories all can be valid without reference to those who express them. A scoundrel can be right. Someone who is unethical can offer sound arguments. Scientific theories can be advanced and demonstrated by men and women who are otherwise detestable. The challenge for you as a student is to be able to listen to and learn from people you don't like or respect— whether teachers, fellow students, or the authors of the books you read. Knowledge often emerges from unlikely sources, and your job as a student is to make sure that you can find and absorb knowledge whatever its origin.

Why is civility such an important foundation of learning?

✔   *Civility tends to breed civility.* It is tough to speak your opinions when your audience is drowning your words with catcalls; it's difficult to refrain from throwing your books at the person who, because he didn't rewind the tapes in the language lab, made you fail the oral test in Spanish. But you have probably noticed that acting as if you expect a courteous hearing before that crowd may sometimes embarrass it to quiet down and that politely asking your fellow student to rewind the tape after using it rather than leaving him a nasty note may bring the results you wish. Probably because of its quiet, unassertive quality, civility is one of the best ways to enhance the conditions under which you can learn from others and help teach them. Anything that contributes to the calm of discussion promotes learning and teaching. And think of it this way: if you're considerate toward others, perhaps you'll be better able to convince them that you're right.

✔   *Civility is in your interest.* Civil conduct (however difficult to summon) implicitly has two goals in view. The first is to allow you to gain something you wish. The second, especially important for a student, is to promote your learning, and that of others, too. Civility is thus one of the surest ways to protect your own welfare and simultaneously to increase your knowledge. If you're uncivil to others, they are likely to be uncivil to you—and that's not going to help you learn.

✔ *Civility comes in all forms, both great and small.* In its grandest form, it implies recognition of all people's right to their own ideas. It means not just acting with consideration toward others but actively protecting others' rights to express their views, even if those views are repugnant to you. That is, civility can mean going to bat for the very principles of formal respect and fairness required for reason to hold sway. You are civil to fellow students, in short, because it's the right way to be. On the other hand, civility may mean simply holding back—not talking too much in class, for example, so that others may offer their views, or letting someone else's harmlessly foolish statement go by without comment. In both cases, civility respects the rules of the game by which discussion and debate take place and from which truth can emerge.

✔ *Civility is an aspect of learning that requires you to think of your responsibility toward others, not just yourself.* Civility looks outward. It asks you to put yourself in others' shoes and to consider what you would want from yourself if you were in their places. You may wish that your fellow student would simply stop making such idiotic statements and keep quiet, you may be tempted to heckle a speaker because you detest the group she represents, but you must ask yourself whether you'd wish others to try to force you to sit down or to prevent you from speaking. Civility is a posture of empathy and compassion, even toward those who inspire feelings of strong disagreement or utter detestation.

Unlike hard work and aspiration, expressive qualities requiring you to reach out from yourself, civility is a more restrained element of studying and learning. It often asks you to repress your impulses and feelings in order to learn what you can from other people. It's no accident that civility is prized in a society that depends upon the observance of certain agreed-upon rules to prosper and progress. Nor is it surprising that schools and colleges insist on civility, for only under conditions of respect and tolerance can new ideas—your own included—take root and flourish.

Yet if civility is part of the "code" by which an open society exists and functions, as well as one of the central norms of your school or college, it is also a personal quality of practical utility to you and your fellow students. It protects your rights to speak and be heard. It protects your access to those sources, including people, from which you can learn. And it protects your opportunities to introduce your own ideas into the universal marketplace of ideas, so that the strongest ones can emerge triumphant in competition with others. In a very special sense, civility is the one personal quality required of all students that enables you to learn what you choose to learn, when and how you choose to do so.

A watchword of civility and of an open society built upon it is a statement attributed to Voltaire: "I disapprove of everything you say, but I will defend to the death your right to say it." It's the principle embedded in the First Amendment of the Bill of Rights, and it should characterize all schools and colleges—and your own attitude toward your studies. Surely it is easier for you to tolerate those who look, dress, act, and think the way you do. But, like your country, you're likely to be judged by the way you tolerate, accommodate, and even learn from those who are not like you, who dissent from conventional opinion, and who hold minority views.

✎

Cynthia Grace was considered the best student in the sophomore class. Her record of A's had yet to be sullied by a single B. Among themselves, her professors called her brilliant. She was destined, they agreed, for influence and success in any occupation she chose. They considered her Rhodes scholarship material.

The trouble was that she thought so too. Most of our private egoistic thoughts are of no interest or harm to anyone, but Cynthia didn't bother to conceal her high estimation of herself. She made clear to people, often in so many words, that she thought herself intellectually gifted. Worse, she behaved toward classmates with an aggressiveness that even her admiring professors found difficult to curb or excuse.

In class discussions, for example, she'd often dismiss others' ideas as "stupid." Rarely content to hear someone else's argument through, she would bully her classmates, interrupting them to interject her own ideas in the middle of what they were trying to say, ridiculing the quality of their arguments, and rarely letting a topic of discussion run its course before shifting it to another subject that she alone wished to talk about. She was known to tell football players that "people who indulge in sports don't have a chance to develop their minds," and she once asked a philosophy professor whether he really knew what he was talking about.

Cynthia became particularly agitated when others refused to listen to what she had to say. She irritated them so much that they closed their minds to her ideas, which to her was simply more evidence of the insufficiency of their brains. "Why should we listen to someone with her attitude?" they wondered. "Even if she's right," one student said, "I wouldn't admit it to her in a million years. Someone who's so stuck-up and nasty probably isn't right anyway."

Acutely aware of the challenge this otherwise intelligent student posed for everyone else (to say nothing of the difficulties she posed for herself), her professors tried to explain the expediency of at least a modest display of courtesy. "Haven't you noticed," they would ask, "that no one wants to listen to you, even when you're correct?" Or, "You've got many good ideas. Could you offer them less pugnaciously? That way, you might convince other students of the validity of what you say." Or, "Perhaps a bulldozer isn't the most constructive implement to use when you want to build understanding."

But all to no avail: Cynthia wouldn't relent in her blistering attacks on others. Her professors couldn't exclude her from their classes—though some wished they could. Instead, like her angry classmates, they hardened themselves to her conduct and hoped she wouldn't take more of their courses.

When it came time in her senior year for her professors to evaluate her character and academic skills for her Rhodes scholarship application, their own reputations for judgment and candor were on the line; they had to tell the truth. Although each agreed that Cynthia was a first-rate student with a mind as powerful as any they'd known in someone her age, none could rate her temperament or conduct so highly. Most of them felt obliged to tell the selection committee in their letters of recommendation that Cynthia wouldn't get as much from the opportunity to study at Oxford as others who were better listeners. Also, she surely wasn't going to improve Anglo-American understanding by the thoughtfulness of her words or the tolerance of her views. As a result, the committee selected others who had less superb academic records than Cynthia's but had learned the lessons of civility that she had considered unworthy of her respect.

What To Do: Admit Ignorance!

Like many people, you may confuse ignorance with stupidity. But the two are not the same. Ignorance is a lack of knowledge, not a weakness of mind; so, while you're never rid of it completely, ignorance can be reduced—through study. Think of ignorance as a friend to learning, for acknowledging what you don't know is a necessary precondition for learning more.

✔ *Don't kid yourself about what you know.* Even if you're a genius, you will never be able to know more than a fraction of what there is to know. So admit to yourself what you don't know. If you pretend you know something but don't, you close your mind to learning it.

✔ *Don't kid others about what you know.* It's foolish, because it keeps you from learning from them. If you tell your teachers that you know something when you don't, they'll move ahead and leave you behind and even more ignorant. But if you admit your ignorance, they'll have the chance to remedy your lack of knowledge.

✔ *Use your ignorance to help determine what you should try to learn.* That way, you're putting your ignorance to use, driving your search for knowledge. Usually, what your teachers want you to learn is what's best for you to know. But they are likely to adjust their approach if you let them in on what you don't understand.

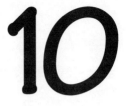

Cooperation

In kindergarten and grade school, your teachers praised you for working well with others, though your cooperative skills then may have been limited to sharing a pair of scissors or a set of finger paints without starting an argument, a fight, or a free-for-all among those other five-year-olds on the floor. The products of the play you were engaged in—the cutouts and paintings—were very much your own, and little of your individuality had to be restrained or sacrificed to the needs of other children so that you could become the wonderful artist you were then intent on becoming and create the early works of genius your parents have kept to this day for your infinite embarrassment. Getting along with other people in school, you were beginning to learn, is not much more than being sociable, and most of us can manage that without undue effort.

But when you grow older and share your scholarly work and artistic creations with others, you are concerned with a quality other than sociability. That quality is cooperation, which, like so many other dimensions of learning, requires active, engaged effort to be of any value.

Cooperation means joining with others, even when you don't wish to, in pursuit of a shared goal. It exposes what you know and don't know to others, even at the risk of embarrassment and criticism, and it contributes your own energy and attention to a shared enterprise so that benefits, sometimes much greater ones, may accrue to others besides yourself. In other words, becoming a student requires giving of yourself as well as receiving from others. That transaction is a hallmark of learning.

This little-noticed fact of reciprocity is basic to all study. You must give of yourself (in the form of knowledge) as well as receive from others (in the form of teaching) not only when you're studying with others in class. You must also extend yourself to people from whom you learn even when they're not present and may in fact be dead—for example, the authors of the books you read and the scientists whose experiments you rerun. Their responsibility to you has been to engage and affect your mind by the clarity, accuracy, plausibility, and force of what they write. Only then are you likely to take in what they offer you. Your responsibility to them is to open yourself to their knowledge and understanding. You must receive what they write, and then, of course, you must evaluate what they say, check it for accuracy, come to your own conclusions, and thus make your own contributions to understanding. It takes two to learn as well as to tango.

Most learning is collaborative and reciprocal. You share what you know and don't know—whether by means of your statements, your questions, your confusions, or your errors—with other students and with your teachers. If you don't do so, you don't learn as much as you can or as well as you might. Nor—and this is what we often forget—do others learn from you.

Being an active member of a class therefore means being engaged and productive in a group that is pursuing the same goal. Only rarely do you have the luxury of having a teacher all to yourself—in, say, one-on-one tutorial sessions; and then your cooperation with those "other persons" is even more essential, because your teachers in such instances must have your full engagement during a session with you if you are to avoid wasting their time and yours. Also, teachers of tutorials aren't likely to miss or tolerate much slackness

Studying Together

Among the great satisfactions of learning is the pleasure of learning together. In classrooms and lecture halls, you often feel alone and at sea, struggling within your own mind to learn, convinced that all the others in the room are following the subject easily and quickly while you're just not smart enough to do so. That's surely not true, but the feelings are real and common. What can you do about them?

One of the best ways to learn is to form a study group—a small collection of people who are trying to learn the same subject. After all, if other "victims" have their support groups, why don't you when you're a student?

To succeed, a study group requires that its members be committed to learning the subject and to helping everyone else learn it. There are many ways to go about that, and here are a few of them:

Read the same material and then discuss it together. That material can be what is assigned in class, or readings on a particular subject that you "assign" yourselves, or just general literature in a broad subject. If it's the last, everyone should be free to read anything that pertains to the topic. That way, each of you brings your own knowledge, as well as information about where to gain more knowledge, to the entire group so that everyone can pursue the matter further.

Discuss a member's paper. There is no reason why,

when you're in high school or college, you shouldn't do what graduate students and professors routinely do—have their work evaluated and criticized before they turn it in for grading or publication. The purpose is not to have the group rewrite the paper but to allow everyone involved in the same project to offer constructive suggestions about the paper's language, arguments, and facts.

Put someone on the "hot seat." This is an especially useful method as exams approach. In effect, each of you is subjected to an oral exam. Self-testing, when you're alone in your room at a desk, can be self-kidding. With an oral exam, each group member's job is to ask hard questions—and, when doing so, to know the answers. In these mock exams, charity is shown by a kind of toughness, for you're all trying to prepare yourselves for the most daunting kind of exam, not for the easiest.

or inattention on your part. So you have no choice but to cooperate if you're to learn.

It may appear to you that even in regular classrooms your cooperation is not essential for the class to proceed well. You may think that what you don't do there has no effect on what occurs, because the results of what is not seen or heard—like the image and sound of a tree falling deep in the forest—are difficult to identify and measure. But that's not the case.

In the first place, when you tune out from what is taking place in class, you deny yourself the chance to learn from your teacher and classmates. In the second place, you deny your fellow students the chance to learn from you. Whenever you say something (whether you're right or wrong, clear or confused, informed or uninformed), you give others the opportunity to learn from the discussion that follows. Whenever you ask a question, you give others occasion to learn from the answer you elicit from someone else, whether your teacher or a classmate.

In the third place, if you've tuned out, you leave the people who are teaching you in the dark about what you know or don't know or understand. You conceal from your teachers the evidence they need to hold your attention, to explain more about what needs explaining, and to find a way to help you learn what you should know. That is, you impede your teacher's attempt to teach you.

To think that the accumulation of knowledge, yours or anyone's, proceeds in a linear fashion—teachers conveying knowledge directly to students—is deeply wrong. You learn through a step forward here, a stumble there, confusion in one place, clarity in the next, one person's lonely efforts here, a group's joint endeavors there, long-unanswered questions in everyone's mind and then sudden, inexplicable illumination in one mind, maybe yours. The search for knowledge is dynamic, complex, often mysterious, and usually surprising—which is why we call the search an adventure. It's like being a tourist keeping a sharp eye out for fear of missing something you may never see again; if you let any opportunity to learn something go by, you may have lost forever the opportunity to learn it.

In fact, when you analyze how you learn, you see how learning works—how often it comes about in disorder, from sudden inspiration or understanding, from the jumble of impressions and facts that compose your mind—and how much it relies on cooperation among everyone. To refuse to join in that complex and irregular enterprise of learning with others is to stop being a student.

Of course, all experienced teachers devise ways to keep you cooperating with them. Some glower at you, others tell jokes to wake you up when you appear tired. Some go around the room and spring questions on you, while others let you drift until you earn a failing grade—an almost certain, if drastic, way to get your attention. In fact, it is one of a teacher's more weighty responsibilities to bring stragglers up to the mark so that all members of a class can learn together. But even when a teacher's discipline is ineffective, your own active efforts to keep the class on track often help to reform the attitudes of your more unengaged classmates. If they see that success with the work brings others satisfaction, they may want to be part of the action, too.

There are times when every student refuses to cooperate with others. Why should you tell those dummies the answers when they haven't lifted a finger to find the answers themselves? Why do you have to listen to that idiot who's always sounding off with stupid questions when you'd learn more if only the professor could get a word in edgewise? Natural questions. You're not expected to suffer fools gladly or without limit, nor is it true that every advance in your learning must take place in concert with others. Often, as we've pointed out, you have to study and learn alone, in solitary, concentrated isolation. But it's true that toleration is as much a part of cooperation as is collaboration.

■

Part of the quality of cooperation in learning, then, is civility: toleration of what you think are the defects in others. It's an axiom of human nature that the imperfections of other people are obvious to us while our own often are invisible. Yet if you are to learn, you have to disregard others' imperfections, or at least keep them in perspective, as you hope others will overlook your own defects.

Your instructor's strange-looking face, for example, shouldn't dominate your thinking about him; you notice it once and then, because he's so good at what he does, you forget it. He is there to teach you psychology, not to win a beauty contest, and his understanding of psychology and his ability to share his enthusiasm for it with you should concern you more urgently than his funny-looking face. Maybe you refer to him by an unflattering nickname behind his back, which is the kind of sport that students have engaged in since Socrates. Sooner or later he'll learn what you call him and be deeply hurt. But what he expects you to do, and what you should expect of yourself, is to get down to learning the psychology he teaches, whatever he may look like.

What are some of the benefits you gain from cooperating with others in the adventure of learning?

✔ *Cooperation introduces you to the minds of others.* Your teachers predominate in most of your learning, for they are older and usually more knowledgeable and experienced than you. They're able to coax thoughts from you that you couldn't have conceived on your own. But your fellow students can do so, too, and their minds work differently from yours. If you work with them, their ideas, which sometimes may seem strange or ridiculous, can open up large new vistas of understanding. So in the right frame of mind, you can learn from other students just as you learn from teachers. Similar rewards await you if you cooperate with the authors of the books you're studying rather than fighting against them. What you learn from them depends largely on your willingness to be receptive, if only initially, to the ideas they present to you.

✔ *Cooperation makes learning easier.* Sharing the work implies that there's a division of labor, so that your portion of it will not be so difficult. After all, it's only fair that you pull your weight. Also, if you pay attention to other students, you may discover that they have difficulty with topics you consider easy, while they find simple what you have to wrestle with. In cooperating with them, you have the chance to explain what you find easy and why, and they're likely to do the same for you. As a result, because everyone's burden is eased, everyone's work gains in quality.

✔ *Paradoxically, cooperation puts you in charge.* If you resist your teachers and fellow students, they have the upper hand, but if you work with them, they have no reason to try to coerce you. You then become your own boss—always a more pleasant condition than working under somebody else's supervision. That way, too, you become your own sharpest critic, meanest questioner, and toughest grader. Your teachers are challenged by your own high expectations, and they consequently teach better. In effect, you are sitting in the educational driver's seat, directing yourself to get where you want to go.

✔ *Cooperation adds human interest to learning.* No matter what your tastes and preferences, you have to be interested in the infinite variety of human nature. Working with others requires you to get to know them as distinct personalities, which adds a new dimension of interest to the subjects you're studying. Of course, you'll like some people better than others, but this means that even a subject you find difficult and unappealing can become attractive because it introduces you to new friends.

Cooperating as a student means adapting your industry to the needs and sensibilities of the other students you study with. That is, the process of cooperating is as important as its results. Sometimes cooperation is a necessary restraint placed on your selfish inclinations, and sometimes it's a necessary reaching-out so that you and others can get something done. Always, it's a personal sacrifice required of you in order to promote a general benefit—everyone's learning.

Cooperation is also likely to make a teacher out of you, because you learn how to assist others to learn. And as every teacher knows, there is no better way to learn and understand a subject than to have to teach it to others. So by becoming your teachers' and fellow students' ally in a common cause, you expand your opportunities to learn and strengthen the chance that what you learn will have meaning for you.

Gary Gordon was twenty-one, but he wasn't as mature as his age. He had worked in a grocery store for two years after graduating from high school, partly to save enough money for college, but mainly to give himself a chance to grow up—or, as he put it, "to find himself."

Gary was far from stupid. He'd managed to maintain a B average in high school, and his SAT scores made him eligible for good colleges and universities. He had never taken up any team sport, but he played tennis well and was a good long-distance runner. What made him difficult was his unwillingness to share any part of himself or his experiences with others.

On the contrary, he was afraid that any working association with other people would mean losing some of the credit he deserved for his knowledge, ideas, and efforts. He guarded his hard-won merits so jealously that they were scarcely evident to anyone. And although he never meant to be nasty to other people, his refusal to respond to overtures from them was usually construed as hostility.

When, after two years of working, Gary registered for college classes, he began his undergraduate studies in the company of students who were two years younger but many years older and wiser when it came to teamwork. Only a few weeks into his first semester he realized that one of the big differences between high school and college was that it was much tougher in this new context to go it alone. At every turn he was pushed into the society of his fellow students. They invited him to join study groups, and two of his professors required their classes to form teams of four or five members each to take up prescribed problems. Sharing a dormitory room with two others made it difficult for him to ignore their lives and keep his own problems to himself. Only by going home every weekend did he manage to give himself even a temporary respite from these unwanted social pressures.

"Why can't they just leave me alone?" he wondered. "What's the big deal about sharing everything? If you shared everything, how would you know for sure what was your own and what was somebody else's?" Gary had so little interest in others' ideas that he would never be guilty of plagiarism. He thus acquired the cheap virtue of resisting a sin that had no temptation for him. And because none of his classmates ever got anywhere close enough to him, he never feared that someone might plagiarize his work.

He got more C's than B's in his freshman year, but he reasoned that college was tougher than high school anyway, so these results were neither unusual nor unexpected. His teachers tried to involve him more in class discussions, but to little effect. Whenever possible, Gary avoided seminars and signed up for large lecture courses in the hope that his preference for solitude would go unnoticed and unpunished. To his dismay, most lecture courses included a provision for small discussion groups, which he considered a waste of everyone's time. He was grateful that in each of his groups other students always had more than enough to contribute, and they effectively hid his silence while he considered them all fools to be so generous with their ideas. He paid little attention to anything they said and so missed much that could have been valuable to him. Two heads, they say, are better than one—but if one of the heads was Gary's, then, the wisdom of the proverb notwithstanding, the other would be ignored anyway.

Gary's selfishness might have been justifiable if it had made him happy. But he pleased neither himself nor other students, who considered him unsociable and reclusive. And of course his failure to work cooperatively with others was no help to him. He didn't really want to live the life of a hermit, and he tried to find work after college, only to be repeatedly disappointed because of the truthful letters his professors felt obliged to write about him to prospective employers. "He is best when working alone and not with others," they wrote. No organization was known to employ such people, and so Gary never made much progress economically or socially.

What To Do: Accept Uncertainty!

Most serious questions, and the answers to them, are complex. Some questions are unanswerable, while others generate many different answers, all possibly good ones. So you have to learn to hold more than one idea, more than one answer—sometimes even irreconcilable ones—in your mind at the same time. This necessary state of intellectual ambiguity is critical to learning.

✔ *Take it as a fact that much is not known—and can't be.* The reason may be because we don't yet have the facts; perhaps it's because our minds aren't up to knowing it. So you have to learn to live with the unknown—as much as you would like to make it the known.

✔ *If you can't answer a question, consider the possibility that it can't be answered.* Your inability to answer it may have nothing to do with the quality of your mind or the intensity of your study. Uncertainty and confusion are often inherent in life itself.

✔ *Doubt others who say they have the answer.* There is no denying that they have one answer. But it's not likely to be the only one. Chances are strong that there are many answers, each one satisfactory to some people but not others, some "correct" for a time but not always. Newton's theory of the universe was "right" for more than two centuries; then Einstein came up with a better idea, which exposed the limitations of Newton's thought.

✔ *Take comfort in uncertainty.* It's a wonderful spur to further study and reflection. Use perplexity as a goad to think more deeply.

11

. . . .

Honesty

You've been told more times than you care to remember that "honesty is the best policy," but seldom, perhaps never, has anyone tried to justify or explain the ancient proverb to you. Nor is it likely that anyone has ever tried to make it directly pertinent to your life as a student, except perhaps to emphasize the penalties applied for cheating or plagiarism.

So what is it that makes honesty so powerful a principle of study and learning? You know that you can be dishonest and avoid detection at least sometimes, so aren't there rewards, you may ask, for hypocrisy, that special kind of dishonesty revealed when you say that you hold to a principle while violating it? Aren't the risks of dishonesty's detection—say, being exposed for copying a paper written by someone else—so slight that being dishonest could well be worthwhile?

Such questions occur to us all, and few of us haven't at one time or another, especially when young, tried to cheat. Yet, as we all found out early in life after stealing a classmate's toy in grade school and then trying to cover up the deed with denials, the mere thought of being exposed publicly for stealing or lying and then having to confess and be punished for it became a powerful deterrent against repeating the offense.

Remember how your teacher humiliated you or telephoned home to your parents?

But we also know that the fear of detection, exposure, and humiliation doesn't work in all cases. After all, we are continually exposed to reports of people in high places who, in spite of being guilty of illegal or immoral behavior, avoid punishment and continue—notoriously, recklessly, and arrogantly—to enjoy the "good life" with impunity. And you probably also know fellow students who have been caught and punished for some infraction of the rules but who have suffered no long-term costs, either because their teachers and school administrators failed to apply the deserved penalties or because the miscreants moved elsewhere with a transcript showing merely their grades. The immunity of such people from suffering the consequences of their dishonesty and their frequent failure to show any remorse when caught persuade many people at best to be cynical about honesty and virtue, at worst to be dishonest.

Of course, you know that dishonesty is not a good idea. But why? Is it for that most sensible of reasons—because you just don't want to have a blemish on your record? Or is it for a worthier reason—because you have a strong conscience and sense of moral right? Both of these motivations for virtue can keep us within the bounds of acceptable conduct, and both are useful deterrents to dishonesty. But for a student, the strongest spur to honesty may have little to do with practicality or morality. For as T. S. Eliot has a character in one of his plays declare,

> The last temptation is the greatest treason:
> To do the right deed for the wrong reason.

In short, honesty is required of you because it's the best way to serve yourself, to help you study and learn. That's the right foundation for honesty when you're a student.

For your purposes, then, the old proverb should read, "Honesty is the best way to learn." If you don't want to learn, then by all means steal, plagiarize, copy, and cheat. Why? Because by borrowing others' words, for example, you are letting your mind stay unexercised and empty; you're keeping yourself from learning to think well.

Consider the matter concretely. If you lift from the Internet the text of a paper on the second law of thermodynamics, you may

Plagiarism

Plagiarism is the scare-word of school and college. It refers to the mortal sin of every student—just short, probably, of murdering one of your teachers (which you may sometimes find equally tempting). It's what you're warned about the first day of college, and it's central to all codes of honor for students. It is the use, without attribution, of someone else's work, passing off as your own the writing, the creation, or the experiment of someone else.

Stealing someone else's work and calling it your own is dishonest. No doubt about that. But it is a particular kind of dishonesty, one that breaches the code by which the world of ideas—the universal community of thought and discovery—works and has to work. "If I have seen further," humbly wrote the great scientist Isaac Newton, "it is by standing upon the shoulders of giants." It is the motto of everyone who struggles to learn and to know: you gain most of the knowledge you possess by struggling to master what others, going before you, have already learned. You stand on their shoulders so that you can learn what they've enabled you to learn and, perhaps, add to what they knew. And so, like Sir Isaac, you should give them credit for what they've taught you.

Plagiarism is a breach of this code. It's the stealing

of intellectual or artistic property. If you plagiarize, you fail to acknowledge another's knowledge, creation, or discovery. If you plagiarize, you don't add to knowledge, you steal it; you don't credit someone else, you falsely credit yourself.

Therefore, the policing of plagiarism has to originate with you. The dangers of detection and penalty may vary, but they're always there. Also, the ceaseless activities of your conscience, knowledgeable about your dishonesty even if you won't admit it, will hound you down the years, giving you no inner peace.

But most important, plagiarism is costly because, if permitted or overlooked, it lessens your own and others' incentives to learn more. Why should I struggle to discover something, you'll be inclined to ask, when someone else is likely to steal it and get credit—or money—for it? Why should I work so hard when that student over there steals my work and gets better grades? The answer is that honesty is the universally shared value that provides the incentive by which knowledge grows, discoveries are made, art is created, and devices are invented.

get a good grade, but you have learned nothing about the law—though learning about it, one assumes, is why you're spending so much time in school or so much money on college. The lazy side of you may of course argue that you just couldn't be bothered to do the work yourself. But plagiarizing runs two risks: discovery and your own apprehension about being caught on the one hand, ignorance on the other. Not bad incentives for being honest. And although the first risk may be the one that deters you from dishonesty, the second one is the more weighty.

How else can you grow through knowledge except by doing all your work yourself? When you were younger, you learned the

multiplication tables, which you still may use in countless circumstances in your life. No one implanted the tables in your mind, like a
pacemaker in a faulty heart. The only way you could use them was
by memorizing them through hard work. In the same way, no one
can slip knowledge of political systems into your brain; nor can you
become fluent in Spanish without memorizing words and phrases, or
master microeconomics without studying the economy. You can fake
some of this knowledge, of course, but when you apply for the Foreign Service or seek a position with a bank, you're not going to succeed without demonstrating that you know your stuff.

The truth is that any standards you follow as a student must
be the high standards you set for yourself and adhere to—not just out
of fear of detection, shame, or punishment, but because those standards are the only ones that protect your freedom to learn effectively.
Vigilance over your ethical conduct doesn't ensure that you'll be the
best student in the world. What it does ensure is that you'll learn all
that you are capable of learning at any particular time because you
are absorbing knowledge for yourself by yourself. Honesty also ensures that you know precisely how well you are doing, because your
instructors are evaluating your work, not the work that someone else
has done.

There's another calculus for measuring the benefits of honesty when you study and learn—comparative assessment. After all,
if you and your fellow students aren't honest in performing the work
you do, how can anyone, either you or your teachers, measure the
progress of your understanding accurately? If the evaluation of the
quality of your work is inflated by its falsity, then the quality of others'
work is proportionately undervalued. By the same token, if others
cheat, you won't realize that you are actually doing much better than
you thought. In both cases, the evaluation of the quality of your own
work is wide of the mark. All students, both honest and dishonest,
suffer the effects of this inaccuracy.

Honesty has many dimensions. It's a social virtue that affects your relationships with those around you. It's a practical virtue that protects you against false assessments of your own capacities. But perhaps most important, it is also an intimate virtue, and its impact inside you is likely to be much more powerful than its external effects. To cheat yourself is probably the most foolish act you can commit, because the ruthless honesty of your conscience will bring you face-to-face with the truth before you can begin to enjoy your fantasy. Kidding yourself that you have studied some course material, that you understand it thoroughly, and that you're ready to face the most challenging test your instructor can devise when in fact you've "borrowed" someone else's work is setting yourself up for an ugly embarrassment when the chickens of your imagination come home to roost in the hard realities of objective assessment.

If telling lies appeals to you in some perverse way, then it's better to tell yourself a useful lie, the kind that the great philosopher Socrates always told himself—that you understand nothing, that you should go back to the beginning of a subject and start learning it from scratch, that you're bound to fail all tests unless you apply all your time and energy to learning. At least in that way you'll work up to your true potential and do as well on tests and papers as you can. If on the contrary you flatter yourself (a popular form of dishonesty, for flattering yourself is really lying to yourself), you'll probably become lazy and neglect the work by which you can learn.

Some people believe that students who think well of themselves are somehow happier than those with lower self-esteem. But unless your estimate of your worth is based on reality and evidence of your achievements, it is no more than a cruel delusion. To believe yourself knowledgeable and competent when you are ignorant is dishonesty headed for disaster as soon as you're put to any kind of test.

After all, education is about knowledge and ignorance. If you know much and if you've worked hard to know it, you can justifiably think well of yourself. But if you're ignorant because you haven't bothered to learn, your low self-esteem is justified—and you shouldn't allow anyone to tell you otherwise. We can't all be "above average." Some of us must be above and some below average in every particular activity, skill, and quality, or there's no such figure as an average. A society in which fools are praised for their cleverness—and in which, praising themselves, people become fools for their self-praise—is like the kingdom of the blind where the one-eyed man is king. Self-esteem doesn't help much in that case.

■

There's another, related kind of honesty that is rarely recognized as such. It's the candor you should expect about your work from others. You should hope that they will tell you the truth about how you are doing so that you can judge best how to remedy your weaknesses and acknowledge your strengths. Furthermore, you should expect them to respect the way you learn best. All of us learn different subjects or activities well, and all of us learn best in different ways—some through words, some visually, some with a special gift for mathematics, others with a remarkable skill in languages. Your years as a student should therefore be seen as part of a journey of self-knowledge in which you devote yourself to discovering how you learn best and what subjects attract your interest most. That's the special honesty reserved for students. When you learn about yourself in that way, your self-esteem will make you truly estimable.

What principles of honesty should you therefore keep in mind as you struggle to learn?

✔ *Honesty means telling the truth about yourself—both to yourself and to others.* Your imagination is always inclined to go into overdrive to present yourself to others in the most favorable light. Often, to buck up your own ego you may succeed in present-ing yourself to yourself in the same favorable, but somehow false, way. Yet exaggerating your true abilities, like minimizing them, is a dangerous step. What you tell yourself about yourself must be the truth. Half-knowledge and self-delusion are no better than a bridge that is "almost secure." Even though it has supported thousands of travelers for years, it may well collapse beneath your feet tomorrow.

✔ *Honesty requires clear-eyed self-evaluation.* The an-cient Greeks summed up human wisdom in two words: know thyself. This naturally follows from the injunction to tell yourself the truth. Self-love is as blind as any other kind of love. As a student, you must learn your weaknesses and failings, as well as your strengths, because only then will you be able to heighten the latter and work to correct the former. It helps to seek the evaluations of others, but in the end, you must rely on your own honest self-assessment. Let others iden-tify your strengths and virtues as a student, as long as you remember that their compliments may be exaggerated for effect. You have to be the detective of your own failings.

✔ *Honesty is the foundation of what you learn.* After all, how can you learn if you can't trust what is in the books you read or what your teachers tell you? How can those who depend upon others' knowledge—astronauts, for example, who rely on both as-trophysicists and engineers for their safety in space—risk their lives if those they trust don't know what they should? All learning depends upon trust—the confidence that what others offer as knowledge is valid and dependable and that it can be subjected to tests and verifi-cation of its accuracy. That's why scientists publish the results of their experiments and why scholars put footnotes in their books—to open their work to the scrutiny and verification of others for its honesty and accuracy.

✔ *Honesty is what others must trust you to exhibit so that they may learn from you.* This is just as important as the trust you place in others. They must depend upon your honesty, just as you must depend upon theirs, as you study and learn with them. If you are dishonest, you may temporarily escape detection, but as the stakes get higher—as, say, you move from hiding an important book from a classmate to falsifying the results of medical research—others can be seriously harmed and a general loss of trust in the dependability of knowledge can result. Your goal should be to learn as much as you can so that others can learn from you, and you should hope that others learn as much as they can from you so that they can extend their knowledge to still more people. Thus the great chain of education extends itself to infinity.

Ultimately, honesty has to do with responsibility. You are expected to take full responsibility for your work as a student and to disavow any work for which you're not responsible. That's why quotation marks and footnotes exist—to indicate what you've borrowed from others, and to pay tribute to those who have gone before you in adding to human knowledge and understanding.

Similarly with your own efforts: if you pay that tribute to others openly by citing their work, then what you add to their work or how you use it freshly can be seen and assessed by everyone. But if you fake it, you're giving credit neither to them nor to yourself. Your merits are then shrouded in a fog of uncertainty and deception.

Then there's the business of living with yourself. Your conscience, that never-quiet inner judge, will be more at peace if you've done your work in the clear light of day than if you haven't. But living at peace with yourself has to do with more than having a free conscience. When you're a student, it has to do with learning the truth about yourself—how you learn, what you know, and what you must seek to know.

✎

Amber Montez met the requirements of her financial aid for college by working in the registrar's office. And most of her "work" consisted of standing in line at the photocopying machine waiting for it to be free so that she could copy what others needed.

As most of us have learned from experience, it's easy to forget to retrieve your original document from a photocopier when your job is finished. So Amber was unsurprised when she lifted the lid one day and found her predecessor's original lying facedown on the glass. She removed it, inserted her own, and started the machine. Then she looked at the other sheet to see whether she could identify its owner. She read the top of the page: "Introductory Calculus Midterm Examination."

Amber was in that course; the midterm was scheduled for the following week; and she was barely passing calculus. The temptation to sneak a look at the exam was palpable, and her dilemma confronted her with immediate clarity. Like all students at her college, she was committed to an honor code that obliged her to return this piece of paper to its owner without reading any more than she had read: its title. Whether the teacher would believe that she had neither read the questions nor (even worse) made a copy of them would have to be his problem.

She could cheat, but the implications of that choice were much more complicated. She would know she was being dishonest to herself, her teacher, and her fellow students. And she'd have to bear the burden of concealment. She could ease that burden by sharing the exam questions either with a few friends or with the entire class. But could she trust everyone to keep the secret as well as she could alone?

And wouldn't some greedy person be stupid enough to turn in a perfect paper and earn a suspicious 100 percent—probably someone who hadn't made a score of anything better than 60 previously? That would ruin it for everyone. But if she kept the answers for herself, she would still face the difficulty of adjusting her responses to show improvement over her own record without making her new level of achievement implausible.

Amber's mind raced through this maze of hard choices without finding a solution. Except one: keep out of this mess by simply returning the paper to the professor. It was he, wasn't it, who deserved to pay the price? She had not done anything to cause this, she thought to herself, and if he didn't believe her, then he'd just have to make up another exam.

She took the original to her teacher, told him she had read no more than the heading, and acknowledged that he might find it difficult to believe her. As she had anticipated, he made up a new midterm, and much to her satisfaction Amber did far better than she had expected. She got a C-plus, not a high grade, but one she'd earned. Surely it felt better than an A achieved dishonestly. And who knows, she thought to herself, perhaps I'd have done worse on the exam I found.

What To Do: Learn Anytime!

There is no best time for learning, but there is probably a best time for you to learn. That might be in the middle of the night or just after breakfast. Convention dictates that study should take place in study halls or after dinner, but convention may not be good for you. After all, isn't the fairest test of your knowledge not when you acquire it but how firm and extensive it is?

✔ *Learn and study when it's best for you.* Just because everyone else goes to the library to study after dinner doesn't mean that you should do so if you're always sleepy then. And don't over-look that quiet hour just after dawn if you're one of those who can jump out of bed and greet the day with a smile—no doubt to the annoyance of your friends.

✔ *Vary the times you study if that will help you learn.* And study different subjects at different times if that works best for you. The purpose of having any kind of study schedule is not to stick to the schedule but to help you learn when you learn best. So keep that schedule flexible if that is best for you.

✔ *Give yourself breaks.* Take a few minutes off every hour. Do something totally different. No one ever said that study must be continuous, only that when you're studying you should be study-ing—and when playing, playing.

12

. . . .

Initiative

Learning requires you to take the initiative for your own education. Because others have helped you learn for so much of your life so far, you may have lost sight of the fact that at no point have they really been able to make you study and learn. Others have prodded you, given you incentives, and helped you in school; but they haven't been able to open your mind to learning. Only you can do that.

Everything you have learned up to now has come because you chose or decided to do so—because you summoned the energy to seize the chance to study and to know. Your science teacher may have shown you how to combine two chemicals to make another and explained how the new one was formed, but only the inclination of your own mind, not the teacher's, got you to absorb that knowledge of chemistry. Your Spanish professor may have given lectures about the medieval culture from which Spanish literature evolved, but you understood those lectures only by reading *Don Quixote* yourself. Therefore, whether you have recognized it or not, you've always been the active agent of your own education.

What are the benefits of taking the initiative as you try to learn? The chief one is the gain to your understanding. By initiating your own learning—by that act alone—you make what you learn immediate to you. What you learn then becomes your own possession. You have committed yourself to learning what you choose to learn, and so your mind works harder and more effectively to absorb what you're learning. This active commitment ensures that you'll study more effectively, reflect more deeply, and understand more fully than you would as a passive student.

Initiative taking is also a form of self-creation. When you take steps to originate your own learning, you help determine many aspects of your life—from what you know, to what you'll be able to do with what you know, to the permanent versatility of your mind, to the endless possibilities open to you to think, act, and grow. Quite simply, you define the person you become.

You may prefer to leave that task to others. But if you do so, you risk becoming the person they wish you to be, not the person of your own choosing—and who knows how that will turn out? Better to have yourself to credit or blame for your life.

Initiative is also a kind of choice. You are the one who decides what your interests are, that you'll pursue them, and how you'll do so. Because learning anything is venturing upon discovering something new, making choices about what you learn or what you concentrate on learning allows you to choose your new directions.

That doesn't mean that no one is going to prod you to embark on your studies, that no one will give you assignments. It doesn't mean that you always know enough to select wisely what to learn and how to learn it. But the initiative you take in defining, even within sometimes narrow limits, your course of study frees you psychologically to learn. You are in command of what you're learning, and your authority over your pursuit of knowledge gives what you learn greater meaning.

Being a self-starting student is also likely to give you much more pleasure and satisfaction than letting yourself be pushed into learning
something. There are few better pleasures than the satisfaction that
comes from learning something new, or something difficult to master, or—even better—something that has never been known before
to anyone, especially if discovering it is something you have set your

Obstacles to Initiative

Two kinds of challenges stand in the way of initiative. One kind is internal and entirely human; it is made up
of such powerful inclinations as laziness, passivity, inertia,
and the fear of taking risks. The other kind of challenge is
external—those barriers that come to exist, often out of the
best intentions and for good reasons, beyond your control.

As a student, you know these external obstacles as
course assignments and curricular requirements, tests and
grades. You love history and want to take another history
course, but because you have to complete a required language course to graduate, you can't fit the history course
into your schedule. Or you want to learn more about fluorides, but your chemistry professor insists that you also learn
about chlorides; to make his determination stick, he assigns
an examination on a subject you don't want to bother learning about.

Rather than accept these obstacles as restraints,
you have alternatives. One, of course—and perhaps the
most effective approach—is to follow your interests outside
class and the curriculum, if you can find the time and energy.
Another approach is to try to "negotiate" a change in your
assignments or requirements to fit your special interests—
say, by explaining to your academic adviser what you think
you'll gain by substituting a history course for a language

course, or making known to your professor your interest in fluorides and the advantages you expect to gain through more study of them, rather than of chlorides. In each case, however, it's up to you to take the steps that will satisfy your preferences.

But what if these approaches don't work? You can try to turn these obstacles into opportunities to learn. If history is your first love among all subjects but you're required to take another language course instead, why not try to select texts in the foreign language you must learn that lead you into the past? After all, you can learn German history in French as well as in English. And if you want to learn more about fluorides than about chlorides, why not extrapolate knowledge about the entire halogen group from what you must learn about chlorides and thus indirectly learn more about fluorides? The trick is to turn a temporary "bad" into a more lasting "good," to redefine an obstacle into an opportunity. If you don't have a choice, what can you lose?

heart on. False modesty shouldn't keep you from feeling the pride that you can and should feel when you've learned something that no one knew before.

Finally, taking the initiative as a student has practical advantages for you. Initiative helps you to stand out above other students who are satisfied merely to learn what they're told to learn and leave it at that. If you have something truly distinctive to offer in knowledge, deeper insights, or fresh ideas, initiative is an essential ingredient in making those known. In other words, taking the initiative in your studies, as in anything else, gives you an opportunity to make known to others what your full capacities and talents are.

So how should you try to think about taking the initiative as a student?

✔ *Initiative taking requires you to define challenges for yourself and to try to meet them alone.* If all you do is take your assignments from others and do the minimum amount of work assigned in a class or required by the curriculum, you're being passive, not taking matters into your own hands to learn. You'll learn something this way, but you won't learn as much as you can or should. To do that, you must create your own goals. Even if they turn out to be similar to your teachers', at least you've thought them through and internalized them, making their achievement personal to yourself. If your goals differ from theirs—especially if yours are more ambitious than those your teachers have set for you—then all the better, for you're more involved in defining your own purposes, and consequently you'll learn more and study more effectively.

✔ *Taking the initiative as a student means anticipating what is ahead.* If you don't seize the initiative, you'll end up constantly reacting to other people's assignments and not putting your own stamp on what you learn and know. Getting ahead of the curve takes work, but it has all sorts of advantages. For one thing, by looking ahead to what you are going to learn, you can understand better what you're learning right now, for you know where you're going. For another, you are in a better position to exploit what you'll learn because you will be able to plan how and where you'll learn it. Finally, looking ahead gives you a chance to influence what you may be asked to learn. After all, why shouldn't you lobby for learning some subjects instead of others—providing you have solid reasons for doing so and can convince your instructors?

✔ *Exercising initiative as a student means running risks.* What are the risks? First, there's the risk of standing out and making others envious. But you shouldn't endanger your own interests because of others' views of you; and anyway, even if you suffer others' suspicions because of your initiative taking, their envy of you is their problem, not yours. A second kind of risk to initiative is the danger that you may mistake the difficulty of the challenges you set for your-self. If you set a goal too lofty for yourself at a particular stage, you may fall short of it and decide, erroneously, that the goal is beyond you. You may then conclude that you can never succeed at what you're trying to achieve. In fact, you probably need simply to work harder, or to make the goal more reasonable, or to seek another way to achieve it. Giving up, even for apparently good reasons, should be your last resort.

✔ *Initiating your own learning sets you up for life.* When you end your formal education, for the first time in your life you become your own teacher. If you are to continue learning, you have to do it yourself. No longer are you going to find teachers, eight or nine months a year, telling you what to learn. Instead, if you're going to learn anything more—from books, art, science, and nature, in addition to the experiences of life itself—you'll have to do it yourself. This is what your teachers have been preparing you for—for life as an independent student and thinker. This is one of the great ends of study: to be able to learn and to contribute to others' learning on your own.

In stressing initiative as the hallmark of a student who is studying and learning as effectively as possible, we don't mean that only you know what's best for yourself, or that you alone should decide what you should learn. Far from it. Others may actually have a clearer and more accurate idea of what you can achieve, what you should seek to strive for, and by what means you should try to reach your goals. After all, that's the assumption behind required courses and the particular curriculum of your school or college—to say nothing of parental care and, for example, the advice of doctors and attorneys.

Nevertheless, there's a critically important role for your own initiatives in your education—for designing your goals and determining your own means to achieve them. It's one of the many ways you can design your adventure of learning—and therefore help design the adventure of life. For only by what you know can you understand life. And your knowledge is determined largely by what you decide to learn.

Constance Soderberg loved school. She never found a course or a teacher she didn't like; they were all "fascinating." She carried out her assignments willingly. She even hated vacations because then she couldn't be in class. Her teachers, predictably, thought her wonderful. Rarely had they had such an obedient, receptive, malleable student in their classes.

But Connie tormented her classmates. She represented all that they were meant to be and weren't. And they disliked her all the more because, naturally, she was what their teachers and parents wanted each of them to be. "Why can't you be like Connie?" their parents demanded. "She does her homework on time. She gets good grades. She's never disobedient. She doesn't challenge her teachers. She does everything they want her to do." This harping from their parents made her classmates look upon Connie with a mixture of envy, loathing, and ridicule.

Many of Connie's classmates seemed to expect everyone to be the same, and they often poked fun at students who stood out for doing something distinctive. They laughed at the girl who spent all her time studying physics, even though they recognized that she excelled at it. They made fun of the boy who took modern dance classes, although they granted that he was a gifted dancer who wouldn't be deterred from taking it up professionally, even if his grades in his other courses suffered because of that determination.

Yet when other students laughed about Connie, they laughed because she didn't have a mind of her own; that was her particular, distinctive trait. They'd never known her to question what a teacher said, complain about homework, propose a project for a class, ask for advice about a subject she said she loved, or even think up subjects for the papers she handed in. Their teachers always had to tell her what to do. Granted, she got good grades, but she was never known to do anything on her own.

When it came time to choose a college—and with her academic record, she had her pick of many—Connie, characteristically, couldn't decide where to go or what to do. But because her teachers had by then discerned her reluctance to assert herself, they deliberately refused to give her advice.

In the first place, they had no idea what, if any, were her genuine interests. In the second, she had made no effort to look into various college programs before the deadline for applying approached. "Why should I do that?" she asked. "Isn't giving me the answer what college counselors are for?" "No," the counselors retorted. "We're here to help you decide where to go after you've thought through the kind of college you want to attend and the subjects you want to pursue. You have to take the first steps." "I don't get it," she complained, in one of her more assertive moods. "I've never had to do that before."

So she continued to be guided by the decisions of others. She applied to one college because her favorite teacher had graduated from there, another because one of her best friends had made a campus visit and was convinced it was the only place for her, and a third because her father said that he would be proud to have a daughter who graduated from it. In this way, she made her "choices" and sent in her application forms.

Not surprisingly, she found herself at the wrong college for the wrong reasons. So she dropped out and started working in a restaurant—a decision that was a bombshell to her parents. They sought advice for themselves and for her and even sent her for some therapy. They had never known their daughter to act like this in her life;

perhaps she was having a breakdown. No, said the therapist, she had just decided at last to take some responsibility for her own life. She, and everyone else, would simply have to get used to that. So Connie enjoyed a break from academic life and prepared herself to make some exciting decisions.

Part Two

· ·

The Circumstances of Learning

13

. . . .

Who Teaches You

You were born to teachers—your parents. Your ability to walk, speak, read, and act with civility is largely thanks to those who guided your first steps and introduced you to a world of wonders and dangers. And beyond your parents and relatives, there were members of the clergy, athletic coaches, and doctors—all more experienced than you—who tried to guide and influence you.

You were still young when you learned to associate the term *teacher* with people who stood in front of you in a classroom and tried to guide you to knowledge. And possibly you came to believe that only the men and women who controlled your progress from grade to grade were teachers. As a result, you may also have come to believe that it was your teachers' responsibility to make you learn. And you may have concluded that your teachers were doing nothing but making your life difficult.

You may still hold these mistaken beliefs. After all, you are not always able to see the benefits of the work your teachers require of you. They expect you to study when you would prefer to do something else. And rarely do they explain to you in compelling terms why you're in class or what's the point of their assignments.

Moreover, though classes and studying are supposed to be the "real" reasons for your attendance at school or college, you probably have other, more immediately appealing reasons to be there: the company of your friends or the chance to "make connections." So

How Should Teachers Help You?

You expect to find certain qualities in your teachers. Your best teachers will have them all. What are they?

Learning. Teachers should know their subjects thoroughly and with enough command to "play" with them —to have independent, substantiated views about them and to be able to engage you in discussing the possibilities and uses of the knowledge they convey to you.

Authority. Teachers should command your respect by the knowledge they possess and the manner in which they convey it. They should create a climate in which you can learn, they should conduct themselves appropriately as people who are, in fact, your superiors in knowledge, and they should succeed in making you aspire to learn by their own bearing toward learning.

Ethics. Teachers should make your welfare as a student their principal concern and responsibility. They should never threaten or harm you. They should be considerate of your own views and aspirations, even if those views and aspirations aren't theirs.

Order. Teachers should maintain the orderly conditions under which you can learn best and should help you learn to discipline your own thinking into orderly processes.

Imagination. Teachers should be able to understand your feelings and situations and to assist you in imagining how the knowledge they are helping you accumulate can enrich your life. They should have a vision of the possible that you may not yet be able to envision for yourself.

Compassion. Teachers should understand and help you overcome the confusions and ignorance that are natural to all students. Because they have gone through what you're now going through, they should be able to put themselves in your place and to acknowledge your struggles to learn.

Patience. Your teachers should give you time to learn, be willing to repeat their efforts, and not exhibit any annoyance they may feel with your confusions and difficulties.

Character. Teachers should bear themselves with the dignity befitting those who teach.

Pleasure. Teachers should convey to you the pleasures and joys they experience in knowing their subjects and help you discover how to gain your own pleasure from what you are learning. They certainly need not always be somber when teaching, for learning often involves wit and laughter as much as seriousness and sobriety.

when you are required to study and learn, you often feel like a prison inmate, held against your will, and therefore you sometimes make the lives of your teachers more difficult. Even though your teachers give you work for your own good, you may experience their assignments as orders, even as punishment. And while your teachers devote their time to ensuring that, as society mandates, you learn a broad range of subjects, you may resent them for not ensuring that every subject you study will get you higher pay or a good job.

So what you gain from your teachers is as much a matter of how you approach them as it is of how they teach you. Surely, therefore, it ought to help you to be a more effective student if you understand who your teachers are, what they are trying to do for you, and why.

For centuries, people have debated whether effective teachers are made or born. Is fine teaching an inherent gift, or is it a capacity that can be learned? We're no closer to answering that question today than we've ever been. But of one thing there's no doubt: teachers can't be distinguished from what they do. Good teachers teach with their whole being. They draw what they offer you from their humanity. Their teaching reveals their selves, weaknesses as well as strengths. And though training and practice can often increase their skills as instructors and minimize those aspects of their personalities that may impede their teaching, each teacher is a distinct "character"—as you've probably already noticed.

Your teachers know that they are bound by an explicit moral contract between you, them, and society. They look out for your welfare by teaching you—and not just by teaching you their subjects. They also have responsibility for your moral development, and those who accept that responsibility are of as much value to you as teachers who are world-renowned experts in their fields. Most teachers take their work seriously, and they mark their success not by the grades you receive or the salaries they are paid but by their conviction that they have struggled as hard as they can to help you learn.

What's more, your best teachers experience what they're doing as a desire from within themselves. They are drawn to teaching because they get great satisfaction from reducing your ignorance, and they embrace as their function helping you to learn. They try to develop your character and enlarge your spirit at the same time they satisfy your hunger for knowledge. In this way, teachers have one of the most demanding and ethically responsible tasks in the world, noble in its aspirations while often exhausting in its execution. It is noble because it is central to the welfare of others who, like you, are typically young and therefore more vulnerable to the world than are adults. It is responsible because on it depends your ability to understand life. Fine teaching is thus a gift of one person to another.

It's a gift not just in the sense that teachers convey to you the results of their knowledge without your paying them directly for it. It's a gift also because the best teachers embody what they're trying to convey to you. They are responsible for passing on to you desirable traits of human conduct—not just by teaching you about those traits but by trying to be examples of those traits in action.

Also, your best teachers have a zest for learning. Certainly they're not seeking fame or fortune; you'll rarely find teachers on the covers of magazines. What they seek above all is your understanding of what they already know, and they're deeply frustrated when, either by their own limitations of ability or, say, your apparent unwillingness to work as hard as they demand of you, they fail in that effort.

Yet while they are not seeking fame or fortune, like actors they hope at least for large and appreciative audiences—not the kind that clap, but the kind that pay attention and learn. Like performing artists, they create from what they know specific, improvised acts of instruction and character—which you then experience as teaching. Some try to win over their audiences (you!) by pandering to them— by doing little except telling jokes or setting low standards and handing out high grades. Most, however, try to win you over simply by struggling to be as good as they can be at what they're trying to do.

Like performers in the presence of their audiences, your teachers *need* you. They don't teach successfully unless you are there to learn. Therefore, it is necessary that teaching and learning be reciprocal—that, like performers and their audiences, teachers and their students become involved in an exchange of minds and spirits, of selves. In that way, teaching is a bit like what we've come to know as "improv" theater—impromptu acts by teachers who are trying to find ways to secure your attention and to add something to your understanding (as well, they hope, as to give you some pleasure).

■

Teachers' individual abilities deeply affect their teaching. Some inspire you in the classroom but can't offer you any useful advice about the papers you hand in. Others lead the most demanding

Teachers Are Human, Too

It is easy to think that the people teaching you are different from you, have feelings foreign to yours, don't know what it's like to be a student. That assumption is wrong. Teachers are human, too.

Your teachers have been students like you. Although they may forget what it was like to be in your shoes, most of the time your presence reminds them of what they once went through. Also, although your teachers are older than you are, sometimes considerably so, they once were young. They can recall what they felt when they were in school or college—and if not, your conduct can always remind them! Most important, your teachers have struggled hard to learn what they know so that they can transmit their knowledge to you.

Your teachers are human in another way, too. Just as you are leading an increasingly complicated life, they too have complicated lives away from the classroom. Like you, they have responsibilities not just to you and your class but to families and friends. They're engaged in other activities and are likely to have other interests besides their professional work. And because life affects them as it affects you, they feel the same range of emotions as you do.

The principal differences between you and your teachers are that they know more than you do about the subjects they teach and that they know both how to convey to you what they know and how to help you learn more about it on your own.

So as long as they are finding ways to teach you and as long as you're learning from them, you have to take them as they are. Although you may think that they're purposely trying to cause you trouble—and sometimes succeeding!—that is not their intention. They are pushing and prodding you, sometimes grumbling and growling at you, because they want you to learn and are often disappointed not just with you but with themselves for not being as successful at teaching you as they wish.

You can—and should—try to forget how your teachers sometimes act and concentrate instead on what they know and say. You can—and should—carefully evaluate their advice, even when it is disagreeable or is delivered in an off-putting way. After all, you're supposed to be studying and learning for your own good, not theirs.

and productive seminars you've ever attended, yet on their feet before a large lecture class they can barely be heard, and what they say is disordered and confusing. Most of your instructors know what they do best. They also know what, because they do it less well, they'd prefer not to do; and some have the opportunity to choose the format of their teaching with that self-awareness in mind.

But here again, good fortune is not always on their side—or yours. The teacher who mumbles must teach the large lecture course on Shakespeare because he's the only Shakespeare scholar on the faculty. The young teacher who would be best teaching the advanced placement chemistry course is relegated to teaching remedial science because the head of her department, a senior member of the faculty, has long taught the AP course, though not very well.

The first person to know that a class isn't learning as it should is usually the teacher, and the teacher usually feels worse than

Knowledge and Moral Good

In the United States, schools and colleges exist for two purposes above all: first, to stock your mind with knowledge and assist you to learn how to use that knowledge so that you can understand life in all its fullness, and second, to help you to be—to assist you to form your character so that you can lead a good life.

Both of these purposes, at their foundation, are moral ends. Yet by saying that schools and colleges have moral missions, we don't mean that learning is religious, or that to be ignorant is to be immoral. We mean that the purposes of a school and a college education are moral because, while the search for knowledge can be (and, at its profoundest, must be) an end in itself, it is also a means to other ends, those attached to understanding the world and living in it. Learning is a moral act because it carries responsibilities to yourself and others.

You frequently hear it said that you must prepare yourself with general knowledge of the world because the world is becoming more complicated and interconnected and changing more quickly each day. Surely there is something to that. But there is a more profound reason for you to possess knowledge: the ethical obligation to know enough so as to be able to make reasoned judgments about your own good and the good of others and to act accordingly.

Just as your own learning bears moral weight, so those who instruct you bear serious responsibilities toward

> you—responsibilities that are communal and civic as well as intellectual and moral. Even while they're teaching you their subjects, they have an obligation to help prepare you through knowledge to take up the role of responsible citizen and community member.
>
> Your teachers are involved in an exchange of knowledge with you that implicitly entails an obligation on both sides—on you to learn and to let others learn, on your teachers to help you learn so that you may lead a good life. They must provide the circumstances—the instruction, libraries and laboratories, serenity, civility, and the like—by which you can learn. If your instructors cannot teach you— if, for instance, you cannot find the books you need, or if there is insufficient quiet or safety for you to learn—you have an obligation to yourself to try to amend these conditions or to see that others amend them for you.

you do about that. Most teachers try their hardest to do the best job they can. The work they do isn't undertaken in secret, and it is subjected to continual evaluations, not only by students like you but also by parents, administrators, and senior colleagues. Few professions are so monitored by so many types of quality control.

Teachers also have different styles, which reflect their different personalities. Some speak deliberately, some swiftly. Some tackle a problem directly, others circle around it. Some are full of gravity while others are witty. Each teacher is likely to have a particular strength or appeal; and so neither you nor your fellow students are likely to find every style of teaching equally effective in advancing your understanding.

There are always these fits and mis-fits between teachers and their students. You have probably experienced both. An alert instructor knows that individual students learn in different ways and that students change the ways they learn at different stages in their education. You learn well in lecture courses because in class you're able to take notes quickly and, outside class, you read in more depth about matters taken up in lectures. On the other hand, your best friend can't stand lectures and will register only for small seminars because she feels more comfortable in presenting her arguments orally and defending them against opposing views. Teachers are the same way. Some are expert in some areas and less expert in others. Just as they have to struggle to find your particular strengths, so you have to work hard to discover and make use of theirs.

Many students see their relationship with their teachers as a tug-of-war, with the students pulling against the teacher's best efforts. This image makes no sense, however, when you stop to think that teachers are trying to help you succeed. If a teacher started each new class by saying, "You're supposed to learn algebra in this class, but I'm going to see to it that nobody learns anything about algebra, and you're all going to get failing grades at the end of the semester," you'd have ample justification for thinking that your teacher was your enemy in a one-sided battle. A metaphor that more accurately describes your relationships with your teachers is that of a see-saw, which works only if the person seated on each end discovers the same, and most appropriate, rhythm for both of you. Then the two of you cooperate to get the most out of the experience.

True teachers—those who give fully of their minds and spirits when they teach you, those who keep abreast of their subjects, and those who are imaginative enough to make something fresh out of what they must teach you each day—know more, preferably much more, than you do about the subjects they teach. While they may not be better people than you are, they are supposed to have knowledge that will benefit you. And they are supposed to know how to present that knowledge to you effectively. You should use their knowledge and skills for all they're worth. They hold the keys to your future.

In other words, good teachers are, by definition, tough

pacesetters. Consequently, being a student often means responding to the demands of teachers you wish you'd never met. They assign a lot of work, they grade it stiffly, and they are always pushing, prodding, exhorting, and sometimes complaining about you as you go about your studies. They may seem like malevolent torturers, but they're not. Their role is to have expectations of you that you may not yet have of yourself.

Although excessive severity or impossible assignments are never good, your teachers are right to have high expectations of you. And they demand that you yield to their superior knowledge and experience—not an easy task in this era of scant respect for authority. But don't you take the medicines your doctor prescribes with confidence and without question? Is it so very different to "swallow" the prescription given you by your teachers and professors?

So your best teachers are those who are unfailingly challenging. They want you to work hard as a way of pulling you ahead. They are a continuing torment to you for *your* good, not theirs. They see the knowledge you accumulate—and, beyond knowledge, understanding—as the key to your future. Perhaps most important, they try to instill in you a competition against yourself, a sense that you must try never to be content with what you know.

And one more thing. Being human, teachers enjoy praise as much as you do. The best kind of praise they can receive as professionals is your acknowledgment that they've taught you something and that you appreciate it. To teach you is, after all, what they aim for, and to hear directly from you that they have succeeded brightens their lives. It may not have occurred to you that brightening the lives of your teachers is one of your functions as a student, but you should give that possibility serious consideration. After all, if your teachers are happy, they may make your life a bit more pleasant, too.

14

. . . .

What You Learn

If you've seen the movie *Ben Hur*, you've learned that ancient Romans enjoyed chariot races the way we enjoy football and basketball—with high intensity and studied excess. And from those Roman chariot races came our word for a prescribed course of academic studies: the "curriculum," which originally meant a horse race.

You may have difficulty relating a chariot contest to your experience in the classroom. Yet because a course can be thought of as a single lap around an arena, the metaphor is appropriate. Also, because athletic trainers and coaches are teachers of a special kind, to identify you, a student, with a sport contestant—best thought of as competing against yourself—makes good sense. Of course, your curriculum may not be as exciting as Ben Hur's races, but winning in your own arena can be exciting and satisfying, too.

At least three considerations lie behind the prescribed courses designed for your studies. One is the presumption, which may or not be true, that you don't yet have enough knowledge or experience to make the best choices when picking courses of study. The second is that schools and colleges operate more efficiently and economically when they can plan for fixed numbers of students, classes, and instructors. If a college faculty decides that English 101 and 102 will be required of all freshmen, the registrar can then estimate how many sections and instructors will be needed to teach the course each year.

But the third and most important consideration has the most cultural weight behind it. It is the ideal of a well-rounded and cultivated mind—the belief that, after studying certain subjects, a person becomes capable of understanding much of the world and of continually learning more about it. Not many people can attain that goal today. Too many subjects have been added to the core curriculum since the ideal was formulated centuries ago, and few people can know more than a fraction of what is now known about the world. Yet the ideal has resisted attack, and it remains the foundation of much of the curriculum.

To explain the comparative stability of school and college curricula, we also have to allow for the difficulty of changing them. Someone once compared reforming a curriculum to moving a graveyard—it's complicated and time-consuming, it offends large numbers of people, and when it's over you haven't accomplished much. That's one reason why the rarely spoken ancient Greek and Latin languages, which for centuries formed the core of the classical curriculum, are still offered in many schools and colleges alongside widely spoken languages like Spanish, French, and Chinese. But there's another, stronger justification for learning those ancient tongues than their place in the classical curriculum: knowledge of their structure and literature provides deep insight into the structure and literature of the English language, which is now the most widely spoken language in the world and whose own structure (like that of every language, as linguists and neuroscientists have learned) has helped create the very fabric of our minds. For these and similar reasons, the idea of the well-rounded, cultivated mind retains its great power.

Distribution requirements—the courses that range through the whole spectrum of the arts-and-sciences curriculum—serve the same purpose of helping you develop a fully informed mind. And behind these distribution requirements is another assumption: that the

The Arts and Sciences

"The arts and sciences," also sometimes called "the liberal arts," is a term that refers to the principal subjects of the high school and undergraduate curricula: languages and literature, philosophy, musicology, and the history of art (together known as the humanities); political science, economics, psychology, and sociology (the social sciences); history (which straddles the line between the humanities and the social sciences); mathematics (a branch of knowledge unto itself); and biology, chemistry, and physics (the natural and physical sciences). They're called the liberal arts because of their liberating capacity, their ability to free you to gain new knowledge—not because they are "liberal" in a political sense. They are what you should be studying in school, and they are what you should aim to study in college if you possibly can.

It is principally in the subjects of the arts and sciences that you are exposed to the broadest amount of knowledge about the greatest range of issues in human affairs. You learn of others' ways of thinking, indeed, of the nature of knowledge itself; of other people in other places at other times and in other circumstances than your own; of the remarkable varieties of human expression in language, literature, art, and music; of the forms and ways of institutions, politics, the economy, and the human mind; and of the incredible wonders of the natural and physical world.

You can't learn as much about these in specialized,

preprofessional majors in, say, business or teaching. So you ought to try to resist if you can any inclination to follow a preprofessional program in college. You ought to try instead, when you're young, to gain the broadest education you can, in the broadest range of subjects that remain strange and unknown to you. That way you open your mind and spirit to the mysteries and complexities of the world. Concentrating and specializing can come later—when you're better educated, older, and more self-knowledgeable.

experience of those who went before you has demonstrated sufficiently (though not without exception) that a curriculum which calls on you to be exposed to a diversity of subjects is most fitting for the development of a wide-ranging and skilled mind.

Even if you are enrolled in a vocational program (like auto mechanics or carpentry) in school or a preprofessional course of study (like premed) in college, you are required to take certain courses and subjects. For reasons similar to those that govern the general arts-and-sciences curriculum, other people already expert in those occupations have determined what you must learn in order to enter them —and they exert their influence by refusing to license or admit you unless you learn what they prescribe. That doesn't mean that the courses for carpentry or medicine never change. Rather, it means that when they do change, you're still required to take the courses prescribed by experts in those occupations. In this way, these occupations assure themselves of the desired preparation and quality of their new recruits.

Thus a large part of the answer to your, and every student's, natural question—why do I have to study this or that?—is that members of the society in which you live and of the institution that you are attending have carefully thought through and made provisions for you to take certain courses and learn certain subjects at this time in your life. Consequently, you have few other options open to you—short of not attending school or college, which we don't recommend.

This overt and deliberate "denial" of your "rights" has many benefits, unlikely as that may seem. If you are struggling with trigonometry, for example, it doesn't help very much to be told that the subject will strengthen your intellectual powers for life and will give you insights into mathematical reasoning, especially if you're heading for law school, where the usefulness of trig has not yet been demonstrated. The truth is that you have no idea what opportunities life may offer you or what twists and turns your career may take, and so there is no way of knowing now what knowledge or skills you'll need and want later. But you can be sure that you'll need the mental strengths that the exercises of trigonometry give you. And so the subject will benefit you after all, at least in that way.

Moreover, most knowledge is "useless" in that it has no apparent or immediate applicability. And so you may scorn it and find little value in it. You may wish that you could take only practical courses that prepare you for a good job instead of those "useless" courses in chemistry or art. But you'll serve yourself better if you bear in mind that knowledge has no end, much of it has no foreseeable outcome, much of it is directed toward the creation of general wisdom, and some of it is simply enjoyable for its own sake.

■

Because of the nature of modern knowledge, you should consider what you study in high school and the first two years of college as an introduction to all that is known. Everything you're exposed to during these six years is, in the larger scale of knowledge, rudimentary. But this doesn't mean that it's unimportant. Quite the contrary.

You are grounding yourself in the intermediate skills of many subjects—going from basic arithmetic to various subjects of more advanced mathematics, for example, and from storybook history to problems of historical causation and analysis. You are familiarizing yourself with many major areas of study—indispensable if you're to make reasoned choices about study, work, and satisfaction in the future. And you are gaining acquaintance with much that is considered necessary for you to know to situate yourself in the contemporary world: basic knowledge of your nation's history, literary classics, fundamental concepts of the sciences and mathematics, and major works of art and music—matters that come up in general conversation and reading. If you are ignorant of these subjects, major areas of life will be closed to you.

It may appear to you as if everything on this curricular menu has been prepared in bite-sized pieces for you to try out, as in a smorgasbord, so that you'll have had a taste of everything this restaurant of a school or college offers before committing yourself to your choice of entree—your major field of study or your profession. But the meal nourishes as well as tantalizes you: by being exposed to many subjects through introductory courses, you test your reactions to these subjects, you identify your strengths and weaknesses, and you begin that most difficult challenge—narrowing your choices of concentration for a major and then for possible postgraduate work.

Meanwhile, plenty of required courses will make you wonder why others have forced their subjects on you. Sometimes the reasons are clear. In high school, for instance, classes in driving and hygiene serve the interests of public safety and health; and your studies of American history and government prepare you for your responsibilities as a citizen. But you may well wonder why you're required to learn French or Spanish. Why not Chinese or Swahili? In fact, why are foreign languages required at all? And in college, when you want to concentrate on studying physics, you chafe at requirements that you take courses in music, art, and the social sciences. Why can't you spend every class hour in the labs?

By requiring you to take a course or two in each of three or four broad categories of subjects—usually the humanities, the arts, the social sciences, and the natural and physical sciences—your college is acknowledging two things. First, it is recognizing that, if you're like most students, you have to be encouraged to range widely across

Choosing Your Courses

It makes little sense to select courses only in those subjects that you already know. You ought instead to try out subjects that are strange to you, dipping in here and there to sample the menu of human knowledge.

There's nothing particularly wrong with following your established preferences and aptitudes. If you know already that you're a hopeless student of languages, for instance, or that you can't stand courses in psychology, there is no loss in steering clear of those subjects. And, especially in college, you don't have to ignore totally the usefulness of courses related to your particular aspirations—although most of what you will need to know for your chosen line of work you'll learn in graduate school or on the job.

But there are other things to keep in mind. One is the reputation of those who teach you. Although spellbinding teachers are no guarantee of a good education, you have to pay some attention to what others have reported about the teachers from among whom you can choose. Registering occasionally for a course because it is taught by a brilliant instructor isn't a bad idea. By doing so, you're likely to see a subject come alive in ways you never imagined.

You should also give priority to your own curiosity. How will you ever know whether a subject might be of interest to you, even fascinating, if you don't experiment—and take the risk of a mistake? After all, this will be the last time you'll have the opportunity to make such cost-free "errors"—though a course "wasted" on an introduction to some subject that turns out to be unappealing to you is not really an error at all. For it has given you greater knowledge of your own strengths and preferences, and you have learned something of another subject along the way. Only by risking—by surprising yourself—can you learn more than you thought you could.

the curriculum. Second, it is accepting the fact that you don't have enough time to take a course in every department or subject. It's hard enough to plan a single course so that you learn what is significant to know about, say, psychology, sociology, or economics; it's even more difficult to schedule you to take a course in *each* of these three subjects. But by requiring you to take at least a single course in one of those fields, your school or college, through its distribution requirements, ensures that you will have some exposure to the social sciences in general.

■

A broader, perhaps a deeper, distribution of courses might be possible were it not for the college major. The purpose of making you select a major field of concentration is to lead you to deepen your understanding of a subject of your choice. The purpose is not, at the college level, to turn you into an expert in it. By asking you to choose a subject and pursue it in depth, the faculty wishes you to get a taste of what it means to know that subject as thoroughly as possible at this time in your life—to become acquainted with its classic texts and issues, to get a glimpse of what it means to be able to "play" with a large subject on your own, perhaps to undertake some research in it.

Sometimes, your major may be in preparation for your future work. Say that you hope to become a biologist and that, to do so, you'll have to attend graduate school in biology. So you major in biology in college to get a head start on what you will have to know anyway and, perhaps, to get a leg up on the competition for entrance into graduate school. Although these are sensible reasons to choose a major, we don't consider them strong ones.

A better principle to guide your choice of a major is to follow your greatest enthusiasm and interest for a particular subject. Because this is possibly the last time in your life when you'll be able to pursue a subject you love without thought of monetary reward or practical payoff, you should let your passion guide you. Do you love music? Before you have to commit yourself to a career, do you want to learn all you can about its history, theory, and performance? A major in musicology is surely the best one for you to choose. You say you don't have enough aptitude to pursue a career as a research physicist and your parents expect you to take over their business, yet you're fascinated by science? Why not major in physics and learn all you can about it before your responsibilities toward your family take charge of your life?

This may seem idealistic; perhaps it is. Many people are forced to prepare early for work and to sacrifice the chance to gain exposure to a wide variety of subjects. But should ideals be thrown out just because tough realities may face you—because, say, your college, parents, classmates, or reality itself is pressuring you into vocational choices that you're not yet prepared to make? One of the functions of ideals is to help you consider what is beyond your immediate circumstance so that you can make reasoned choices appropriate to you. Therefore, your major field of study ought ideally to be the field that most captivates you, that most grips your mind and spirit during the last two years of college.

In addition, the idealistic approach may turn out to have large practical dividends later on. In contemporary society, people who can range widely over many subjects, who command many perspectives on the day's issues, and who possess skills in numerous ways of thinking—all the strengths a general education in the arts and sciences is designed to give you—are increasingly valued. So while pursuing a "useless" major in college may seem a luxury that can be enjoyed only by privileged students, later on it may yield great benefits in increased opportunities for you, greater authority in your occupation, and greater respect for your ability to face the challenges of your chosen work.

Your major should be your choice for *your* reasons, not others'. When you choose it, you can throw yourself into it better than if it has been forced upon you. And then you are living up to your college's hopes for you—that you will abandon yourself briefly to a single subject and discover the great joys of learning about something deeply and well. There can be no better capstone to a college education than that.

What To Do: Learn Anywhere!

Just as there are no rules governing when you should learn, so there aren't any rules governing where you should do so. What counts is what you learn, not where you learn it. You have to learn wherever doing so works best for you—at the beach, off in the corner of a fast-food restaurant, in the doctor's waiting room, or in the car (preferably as a passenger). You'll find that you can learn in the most unlikely places.

✔ *Figure out where you learn and study best.* Try out different places, different circumstances. Seek others' advice, but don't exclude places some might think unusual.

✔ *Change where you learn if that will help you learn.* You change, and your moods vary. So why must you study and learn in the same places all the time? Try varying the places where you learn different subjects. One subject is best for the library, another for the backyard. You don't have to be consistent, but you do need to find out what works best for you.

✔ *If you need privacy for study (and most of us do),* prevent others from finding out where you go to learn. Friends will respect your need to get away from interruptions. Those who don't respect it aren't good friends—or perhaps good students.

15

. . . .

How You Learn

The circumstances in which you learn often appear beyond your control. Your teachers call the shots in their classrooms and lecture halls—telling you what you must learn, assigning homework you must do, and grading the papers and exams you must complete. Even when you're away from them, you still feel their influence on your life. You have to do *their* homework; you have to study for *their* exams; you have to prepare *their* papers and lab reports, play the music or act the scenes *they* assign, sketch the object *they* require you to draw. Is there no escape from their dominating presence? Can't you be free to do what you want?

Well, to some extent you can be—and in a way that's essential to your welfare as a student. You can control the climate for your own learning even if you can't control everything that you're told to learn. You can figure out how to take advantage of what your instructors offer you, or you can get by with the minimum amount of work carried out in the least suitable ways. Although you may never be fully in command of your own life as a student, you can decide how to approach your forced educational labor and get close to controlling it.

You've been told that regular, orderly habits of study help you succeed as a student—sitting upright at a desk, for example, and keeping to the same schedule of after-class homework (two hours before dinner, say, and two hours after). They may do so. But the trouble

Grades

Grades are evaluations of your work, not of your character or intelligence. You may be a wonderful person but a failure as a biologist. You may find it impossible to do satisfactory work in history but may excel in all other subjects. Grades are meant to illustrate these distinctions for you and others. After all, you don't want to become a doctor (nor do your prospective patients want you to treat them!) if you fail every subject in medical school. In such an extreme case, bad grades serve the purpose of ensuring that you choose another occupation.

Furthermore, your teachers grade only the work that you submit. Their responsibilities are confined to single subjects and single courses. That, after all, is their area of expertise. Your English teacher cannot judge your work in chemistry. And a professor who marks you down because of your political beliefs is both unprofessional and unethical.

Human concerns affect your teachers as well. They don't want to give you low grades, and they don't want you to dislike them because of those grades. They are as determined as you should be that you will do as well as you can. But to do well, you have to cooperate with them in the adventure of learning. You have to exhibit evidence that you're doing the work they ask of you, that you comprehend a reasonable proportion of it, and that you are meeting the standards for achievement of the level at which you're studying. If you do that, your teachers have no reason to fail you and every reason to give you respectable grades. If you don't do that—well, grades are incentives to encourage you to do so.

If, as hard as you try, you simply can't understand a subject and can't earn a good grade in it, take some consolation that there's no clear link between doing well in school or college and leading a good life. Who ever said you couldn't overcome a bad academic record, or that those who get the richest fellowships or the best jobs lead happy and easy lives? Consider Winston Churchill's school reports during his years at Harrow, his secondary school. Most of Churchill's teachers agreed that he was a teenager of little promise. Yet he went on to become First Lord of the Admiralty and prime minister of the United Kingdom during the Second World War—one of the greatest prime ministers, in fact, in British history.

with such advice is that it fails to recognize that the ways you study and learn have to suit you and nobody else.

Sitting upright at a desk won't work if you have no desk, and following a fixed schedule of study makes no sense if other responsibilities won't permit it. Yet if you adopt ways of study that are different from those conventionally advised, you ought to have solid reasons for doing so. Cramming for an exam for three hours after a night of partying, for example, is not an ideal way to learn—or to do well on the exam. Even if all conventional wisdom doesn't work for you, there is no reason why you can't try to adopt some of the approaches—such as studying in a quiet place—that others urge upon you. You have to find the most effective ways to study and learn. Whatever ways work best for you are the ones you should use.

Unless you are asleep or unconscious on a hospital operating table, you can study anywhere and at any time of the day or night. Even if you haven't tried to study at 3 a.m. or at a football game (and we don't particularly recommend either), you've probably noticed others doing so, and some of them probably do reasonably well in their work. If you already know your own inclinations and most successful methods of studying, you should certainly indulge them, as long as they help you attain your main goal—the maximum of learning you can achieve. You may like some background noise or music, for instance, or perhaps their opposite, absolute silence. Perhaps you study best sitting at a desk, perhaps in an easy chair or spread out on a sofa. Perhaps you require solitude, or perhaps you need the company of others at the library. The possibilities are endless, but the purpose is always one and the same: to get your work done as effectively as possible.

This is common sense, and you may therefore decide that it's not worth thinking about. But ignoring it won't make it happen. If you make a list of the conditions under which you study best, then consider how frequently in the past month you have tried to cultivate them, perhaps you'll see a problem. For most of us, it's hard to make the effort, and taking the time may be too much bother. But practice usually brings rewards.

Consider a classic situation: You have your own desk, perhaps in your bedroom at home, possibly elsewhere. At some point, a parent tells you to go to your desk and sit down and do your homework. So, feeling lonely and generally rather sorry for yourself, you go and sit there, but you really want to talk on the phone with your friends. You dutifully get out your books and papers and make a start at what you're supposed to be doing. But then, a few minutes later, your mind wandering, you turn on the radio to find some music. You spot a magazine across the room that you haven't read, and you turn away from your assignments. Before you know it, an hour has gone by, and you've barely cracked a book. Soon, your parent, assuming that your homework is well along and thinking that you've been without company long enough, calls you to dinner. And that's that. You haven't finished your assignments, but at least no one plans to force you to do it, and you're not stuck in your room any longer.

The habits established by such a pattern are usually harmful. You associate them with the punishment of being sent to your room, with doing something you don't want to do, and with being cut off from your friends. These negative associations are likely to affect the way you approach hard work and learning for the rest of your life. Almost any alternative to studying will be preferable. Years later, you may still think that studying means subjecting yourself to the same conditions you endured as a child, to suffering some kind of coercion. So when you find yourself at college sharing a room with two other students who are always enjoying a party when you're trying to study, you are likely to succumb to those old feelings and to put aside what you should be doing. Unpleasant associations are hard to break. If you're going to study and learn effectively, you'll have to review, even recast entirely, the way you think about studying—always tough work.

There are no prescriptions for studying, no rules, no surefire ways to straight A's. Human personality is too complex and students like you too diverse to ensure that what works for someone else will work for you. Like so much else related to studying and learning, experimentation—your active engagement in your own studies—is the key to learning how you can become the best student you can be. Yet experimentation is the key, as long as you keep your eye on two closely related goals—the first, to achieve a genuinely workable approach to studying and learning, the second, to be true to yourself.

Authenticity in learning doesn't mean that the ways in which you study should be unvarying from day to day or unchanging as you yourself change, nor does it mean that the way you study for one subject should determine how you study for another. But by the same token authenticity doesn't mean that anything goes— that you're justified or well served by studying any way you feel like studying. Instead, it means that you try consciously to figure out what works best for you and no one else. In doing so, however, you ought to seek some sort of balance between your momentary moods and your more enduring interests, some middle way between personal idiosyncrasies and rule-book certainties.

Those moods and interests are likely to be very much affected by the environment in which you try to study, the disposition you bring to your studying, and the condition you're in once you get down to hard work.

Let's take the environment for your studying first. Only you can say where you study best. If you find a carrel in the library too quiet, perhaps you'd do better at a table in the cafeteria—as long as you can keep intrusions away and close your ears to interruptions. If you like to study surrounded by your friends, you may do well in the main reading room of your school or town library—as long as you're all at work. You may like sitting outside, as some people do, or even like reading while walking—a practice safer in the past than in the contemporary world of cars, bicycles, and rollerblades. Like most matters regarding learning, the surroundings in which you study are worth conscious thought and planning. It makes no sense simply to fall into settings that are contrary to what you want or need.

Yet the best and most suitable conditions for studying involve more than just your immediate environment. They also involve your own disposition. You have to be prepared for the work at hand. You have to get yourself in the appropriate frame of mind. Like discovering the places you study best, the way to create the right mood for studying is not something that's taught; you have to figure it out for yourself over time. It is the state you want to get to in order to make the best use of your time and energy. Some call it "focus"; in sports, it's "the zone." Some people achieve it through yogalike meditation, others by simple force of concentration—"Come what may, I'm just going to sit down and do this." But however you do it—and your approach may differ from one time to the next—getting yourself ready to study is essential.

A third condition affects your studying: your physical state. Here again, the rule books are clear: plenty of sleep, balanced nutrition, hunger satisfied, sobriety, and decent physical health. But that's not all that is needed. To borrow another metaphor from physical sports, you probably also have to "train" for studying and learning. You have to practice how to do it, starting with short periods of study and building up to longer ones, to get so that you can quickly get up a head of steam. Eventually, you'll reach the point where you are in such good shape that you fall into studying without much preparation —even, perhaps, under the worst of conditions and in the worst of moods, much as athletes sometimes do when they have to compete.

Fortunately one of the best conditions for study—after you've taken care of your surroundings, put yourself in the mood, trained yourself into condition, and then actually applied yourself to the work—is relaxation, both between and after your work. No one has ever said—at least not sensibly so—that you have to exhaust yourself or deny yourself every pleasure in studying. In fact, breaks between bouts of hard work and periods of complete relaxation afterward are as important to your success as a student as they are to the effectiveness and peace of mind of athletes, laborers, and soldiers. Just as combat can break one's mind and unrelieved work can destroy one's health, so unbroken study can quickly dissipate all that's been gained by unbroken effort. Your mind becomes confused, you forget what you've learned, and everything about learning becomes distasteful.

So you have to find those ways in which you can best get some rest and break free of the hard work of learning. You have to learn the difference between your natural laziness and your inclination to be distracted on the one hand and the genuine need on the other to switch gears, take a new approach, or move on to another book or assignment—anything to revive your flagging interest and keep yourself up to the mark. A good beginning may get you a long way toward your goal, but it's staying power that achieves enduring results—and staying power must always be recharged by good old-fashioned relaxation.

Other, basic principles about the conditions under which you study and learn should also be kept in mind.

The first is that how you study is as important as what you study. To be interested enough in a subject to want to learn about it without knowing how doesn't make much sense. Different subjects require different approaches to learning, and perhaps different conditions. After all, you don't study poetry in a physics laboratory, nor chemistry in an art studio. Similarly, reading is likely to require different conditions than a subject, like musical performance or dramatic acting, that demands practice space. So your approach to studying can determine what you learn as much as the subject you're trying to learn.

The second principle is that because studying is always a challenge, you might as well accept it as one. Learning what you must learn—as we've repeated often—is rarely easy; nor is getting yourself to study usually a breeze. Instead, studying often involves gritting your teeth, postponing more immediate pleasures, and putting yourself through the frustrations of making your stubborn brain work the way you want it to. That is precisely the point, for if it were easy, there wouldn't be a need to put yourself through those torments. It is therefore essential to have a realistic view of what it takes to study—perseverance, application, and what the Germans call *sitzfleisch*, or applying the seat of your pants to the seat of your chair.

A third principle is that the conditions under which you study cannot do away with the difficulties of study. But then eliminating them is not the point. You are trying to make the best use of the time and effort you have to put in anyway. Those old rules about sitting at a desk in a quiet room are not intended to help you feel comfortable when you're memorizing French verbs, and they can't make learning differential calculus any easier. But following such advice can speed your learning and allow you to get on to other efforts you ought to be pursuing—which may, of course, include more studying.

Finally, the conditions of study can't be, and perhaps shouldn't be, unchanging. The subjects you study, the places and moods you're in when you do so, and the time you have to carry out your work all vary, sometimes from minute to minute. In addition, you can be interrupted against your will; complications in your life can force you to fall behind and then to make up work quickly under taxing circumstances; you can become exhausted and be unfit for learning because of excessive demands made on you. Studying thus usually requires flexibility, trials (and inevitable errors), submission to the imperfect, and—always—your determined efforts to get back to the conditions under which you study best.

The ideal situation for every student is a clear mind, a rested body, a good subject, congenial surroundings, and the opportunity to enforce on the rest of the world what should be every student's best defense against intrusion and interruption, one with no need of further justification: "I'm studying." Rarely, however, are you likely to enjoy all these ideal conditions at the same time.

To summon the best conditions from imperfect ones may require you to set fresh and challenging goals, whose attainment brings you the greatest satisfaction—to try studying alone, for example, when solo performances are not your usual way. It may require you to set reasonable benchmarks for each occasion you study, like milestones to reach on a journey. But whatever the case, you can't expect others to provide you with all the circumstances you need for learning. You have to create them yourself.

What To Do: Evaluate Yourself!

Your teachers shouldn't be the only ones who examine you and evaluate your work. You should do that, too. It's a good way to take the initiative and monopoly of testing out of their hands, and it's safer. For the quiet voice inside you can often be more honest about your work than others are.

✔ *Be honest to yourself about yourself.* If you kid yourself about what you know or how well you study, then what's the use of the time you spend in self-assessment? The privacy of your own mind keeps the outside world ignorant about the grades you give yourself. So make sure they're accurate.

✔ *Hold yourself accountable for your shortcomings.* Don't blame others for what you don't know. And keep in mind the great practical value of responsibility. You can head off others' criticisms if you recognize and work to correct your shortcomings before they do so.

✔ *Give yourself credit for your strengths.* There's no purpose in being too hard on yourself. Don't give way to pride or arrogance, but learn and acknowledge what your strengths are. They're all you have to go on.

✔ *Check the accuracy of your self-evaluation against the standards of others.* Most people can't see themselves clearly. So your view of yourself is likely to be prejudiced—either too favorable or too critical. Seek the evaluation of others to help you judge yourself accurately.

16

. . . .

From School to College

Many students complete their formal education with high school, and you may be one of them. Or perhaps you are going to postpone entering college until you've put some money aside or gotten a start on your career. If you're not going on to college, at least not directly, you may safely ignore what we say in this chapter. Yet we think its subject worth your attention whatever your plans. Certainly, we recognize that going from high school directly into the world of full-time work and responsibility is a great and important transition, one for which as much preparation is needed as for the move from high school to college. Yet it's a different subject altogether. And because it's so different, we shall say nothing further about it here.

This chapter is about that other option that is open to you when you leave school—the transition from school to college. Like taking up full-time work after you receive your high school diploma, enrolling in college marks a major transition from dependence to independence, from adolescence to adulthood, from others' hopes for you to your own hopes for yourself. The change doesn't happen all at once. For some it takes more time than for others. But much of it occurs during your college years. The choices you make from the time you enter college, like other choices you may already have made in high school, have real and often permanent effects on your life. They shape your character, your career, your sense of self, and your knowledge of the

Is Knowledge All?

Should the goal of learning stop with knowledge alone? Are there other kinds of learning besides knowledge that we should hope to develop and possess as we study and learn, even if we can't develop them by study alone? And can the pursuit of learning lead to something beyond knowledge? The answer to these questions is surely yes. For just as knowledge is distinguishable from information, so it is distinguishable from other human capacities that reach beyond knowledge.

It is often said that knowledge can be—some say that it should be—an end in itself, something we acquire for the sheer love of learning, but human knowledge comes fully into its own only when it is put to the service of human qualities that result from the acquisition of knowledge. The first of these additional qualities is understanding—knowledge given meaning. You may know all there is to know about the vast and complex series of events that made up the American Revolution, for instance, without comprehending why the revolution occurred or what difference its occurrence made to American history. Understanding can be seen as knowledge applied to some question or problem in order to explain it and impart significance to that knowledge.

And even understanding is not the final end of knowledge. That's reserved for a second quality: wisdom—the quality of sound, reflective judgment about ends and means, about the good and the bad, through experience and reflection, often through intuition and faith as well. We all wish to be smart—to possess native intelligence—but we should all hope to be wise as well, to have discerning and sound judgment about the challenges of life.

The aim of a school and a college education, then, is not just to make you knowledgeable. It is to set you on a course to understanding and wisdom through the knowledge you begin to obtain when you study and learn.

world. So entering college is a benchmark in growing up. It's also an important occasion to remeasure yourself and to do so through study and reflection.

During your school years, you are kept pretty much under watch—for your own benefit—by your teachers and members of the school staff, then at home by your family. By contrast, at college you're left much more on your own. You are expected to know your own mind or to be able to seek the advice you need from those who can best help you decide what to do. You are also assumed to have enrolled in college so that you can take advantage of a college education (though too many students attend college for less worthy reasons).

If it turns out that you're not prepared to make full use of that opportunity, there are fewer people holding out safety nets for you and protecting you from your own misjudgments or missteps. Out of school and often away from home, you have no one constantly prodding you to take the initiative, to work harder, or to aspire higher. Your own native or developed traits of character now determine whether or not you can make the most of what is being offered. You're much freer to make mistakes, to make them on your own, and to pay the costs of doing so.

In addition to these novel realities, you are probably living away from your family for the first time. You reside among people you've just met, in unfamiliar circumstances, and without the known and expected responses from others that you could anticipate and depend on at home and school. You may also be away for the first time from old friends, those with whom you've grown up, and without their immediate affection and support you are fully reliant for the first time on yourself or on the kindness of strangers. Suddenly, self-reliance becomes your major resource.

Equally important—and this happens so gradually that you may not notice it—you shift away from others' expectations for you to the compass setting you establish for yourself. Now your orientation must be your own, the directions you go those of your own choosing, the decisions you make your own responsibility. This is a time in your life of heightened self-definition and commitments.

Because all these normal developments in the modern human life cycle coincide roughly with your years in college, your college education is designed to encourage you to integrate your intensified understanding of the world with the completion of your maturation into an adult. Study and learning contribute to your growing sense of self. Equally so, your growing sense of self is expected to contribute to your education. What is called your education now becomes, in reality, your self-education.

■

Because so much rides on your years in college, the transition to collegiate life and responsibilities may test you to the utmost. And at first it may not be the appealing situation that others have made it out to be. Instead of finding your life easier and more pleasurable because now you're free of earlier restrictions, you find yourself alone. Feelings of homesickness, confusion, sometimes outright desperation may flood in upon you. Waves of uncertainty wash over you—Can I really succeed at this? Do I really want to be here? Occasionally you feel like dropping out and running home.

Sometimes, too, you are ashamed of your own confusions. You may be tempted to use your newfound freedom to engage in activities that you couldn't get away with at home, and you feel a combination of guilt and anxiety about the consequences of what you're doing. And then you're asked to make up your own mind about innumerable matters of which you have little knowledge and less experience. What courses should you take? Who among your new acquaintances, faculty members and students alike, deserves your trust? How can you coordinate the needs to study, to earn some money, and to relax? What should be the balance between your studies and the attractions of extracurricular activities? Can you really do all this?

The people you used to turn to for help with these matters are no longer readily available; and, anyway, they may not know much about your situation. After all, you may be preparing to attend —perhaps you are already attending—a different kind of institution than your parents attended. They may not understand your curricular interests—why, for example, you want to study art history when a prelaw program would prepare you for greater income in the future, or why you want to major in physics when accounting would better equip you to take over the family business. In any case, they can't help you much in deciding which courses to take during freshman year or in figuring out whether the staff of this or that student newspaper is the best one for you to join as you prepare for a career in journalism.

If you are more on your own in college in making these kinds of decisions, you're similarly on your own in your studies. Through high school, you were expected to learn from your teachers. It's a good rule of thumb that in ninth grade roughly 80 percent of your learning comes from your teachers and the remainder from your own study. That proportion gradually changes through high school. You rely increasingly on your own study and on your classmates, until your teachers contribute perhaps 60 percent of your learning. Then in college, the proportions shift sharply; your professors provide you much-needed direction, but most of your learning now comes from your own solitary work and from conversations and study with your fellow students.

Also, if you're taking full advantage of college, much of what you learn by yourself will be spurred by your own interests and the recommendations of other students, as well as by the subjects of your courses or the assignments in them. The most enduring knowledge and the most significant intellectual sources of your mature attitudes often originate in the excitement of informal collegiate readings and in conversations about matters that are new to you. You ought to embrace such opportunities with enthusiasm.

If all this confuses you, it may be some consolation to know that you are not alone in your bewilderment. Your fellow students— who may strut about with such apparent confidence, who appear so eager to get out of high school and embrace the independent life of a college student, and who seem so much at home the first day of college—likely feel the same strains and anxiety. They're just better at masking those feelings—and they may think that you're the one with all the answers. Some of them will quickly make mistakes that will affect their lives long afterward—throwing themselves, for instance, into the drinking and partying ways of fraternities and sororities, or taking lots of "gut" or preprofessional courses rather than a solid grounding in the arts and sciences. There's no need to envy their bearing or imitate their actions. They may appear the very picture of poise and security, but inside they are probably feeling as insecure and uncertain as you.

In addition to remembering that the transition from school to college is a rough one for most people, attended by a certain irreducible amount of perplexity and anxiety, you should bear in mind that the transition also requires time, often more than a year, to complete. To fear mistakes (about everything from applying to college to registering for courses), to wonder whether you're going to the right college or doing what is most appropriate for you—these are normal feelings and quite possibly productive ones, for such concerns reduce the temptation toward complacency. Your confusions also test your capacity to make the best use of this new stage in your life, when you move, as a student, from youth to adult responsibilities and independence.

In fact, that is the crucial challenge: can you make the most of your extraordinary opportunity to attend college, to learn more widely and deeply than you've ever learned before? These years are the last time in your life when you will be able to focus on developing yourself and yourself alone. After college, you'll have to go to work and take up other adult responsibilities. This is the last time when others are likely to approve and accept such selfishness and self-regard on your part.

■

Given the complexity of your move from school to college and the weight of the decisions you must make, it helps to keep in mind some considerations about making the transition.

Because choosing which college you'll attend is perhaps the most important decision you'll make, that selection requires deliberate and clear thinking. Yet students, parents, and guidance counselors frequently make serious errors about college choice. The best reasons for choosing a college concern the quality and extent of its programs, its "fit" for you, and your ability to make best use of what it offers. Such matters as an institution's distance from your home, its local reputation, the quality of its football team, or the fact that your best friend is going there must be of secondary importance at most.

In a choice that is going to affect your entire life, shouldn't you make the decision on the right grounds?

Not all economics departments and engineering schools, for example, are of the same quality. If the best one is also the farthest from your home, it probably makes sense to struggle to find the extra $500 for travel there than to attend the weaker and closer one. Similarly, preferring to attend X University rather than Y University because of the winning streak of X's basketball team is among the poorest reasons to make a choice, particularly if your ambition is to be a biologist and Y has by far the stronger biology department. Nor should such considerations as where your parents went to college or where your current boyfriend or girlfriend plans to go play much of a role in your decision. You ought to attend the college that is best for you.

As you prepare for the transition from school to college, you should also prepare yourself for what is likely to be a rocky start. The first days of registration and course enrollment are filled with herdlike movements, the pressure for speedy decisions, and the confusions of a new life. And before long you are attending courses whose subjects and approaches differ from any you've taken before. Even high school valedictorians find that college courses are more demanding and academic expectations much higher than in high school—often to their discouragement, when their previous A's turn into B's or worse. Having some distance on yourself, knowing that what you're going through is normal, may help you to weather the difficult months of your first year.

You ought also to take some comfort from the fact that almost all your peers experience the same feelings. Everyone feels lost on campus and confused about courses and expectations. So besides struggling to keep your wits about you in this new and strange world, the most important step you can take in your own behalf is to concentrate on selecting the best courses, from among both required and elective courses, that are appropriate for you. In fact, you can do nothing better than to use your energies to sound out your own mind, consult faculty members and advisers who can best help you make wise decisions, and give yourself the time and circumstances to make those decisions. As long as you are well anchored in your academic life, the rest will eventually fall into place.

Registering at college therefore means more than changing your place of residence or work. It means reorienting the way you think about learning. Although you are the same person in college as you were in high school, you soon feel differently about yourself, and that difference should enable you to be a different kind of student.

It is also essential to keep in mind that, despite what others may say, college is definitely a part of the "real world." In the single sense that it should be a place for deep learning, quiet reflection, and unrestricted thinking, colleges do in fact differ from much of the rest of the world. But to suggest that a place where one learns to think well and learn deeply, where you have time to make some of the most important decisions of your life, is somehow cut off from the rest of the world is thoroughly mistaken and hopelessly cynical. To believe that college is outside the world is to believe that clear thought and wide knowledge have no place in life, when all evidence is to the contrary.

At college you are part of the world, not only in the sense that those with whom you deal there—students, faculty members, and others—are human beings just like everyone else, but also in the sense that what you're learning there, whether accounting or literature, prepares you for your full role as adult, worker, and citizen. To think of college as a four-year vacation from responsibility—both to yourself and others—is to waste your time and money.

Preparing for and making the transition from school to college should call into play all your best and most deliberate thinking. If it does so, you set yourself up for college years rich in learning and fulfillment. And if you make the transition effectively, you can then concentrate your efforts on developing the qualities and dispositions by which you can make the most of your extraordinary chance to learn.

17

. . . .

Some Final Thoughts

Throughout this book, we have urged you to be a student in the fullest sense of the term by developing and using some of the qualities you already possess. We have also done all we can to persuade you that employing these qualities is infinitely more rewarding than not using them and simply pretending to be a student.

A line from Wallace Stevens's poem "The Emperor of Ice Cream," which we quoted earlier, summarizes our meaning exactly:

Let be be finale of seem.

In other words, we urge you to make *being* a student replace *seeming to be* a student if you are to benefit from your education. Pretending to learn leads to ignorance and error; only real learning produces knowledge and understanding.

You may remember a remark by Elliott, in the movie *E.T.*, when he was asked whether he'd told the extraterrestrial creature hidden in his house about school: "How do you explain school to a higher intelligence?"

You may share Elliott's conviction that schools and colleges are beyond explanation. But even if you could explain them, it wouldn't help you succeed as a student, because what makes you a successful student is not your understanding of the educational system but rather your understanding of what is already within your grasp—your own human characteristics and how to use them.

The characteristics you need to be a student are far more important than how well or badly the institution in which you're enrolled helps you to be one. If you try hard enough and in the right spirit, you can achieve your goals despite circumstances that may impede you. No matter how bad their teachers or how negligent their schools or colleges may have been, individual students have always managed to learn and grow. This is one of the great unheralded triumphs of the human spirit. These students have succeeded against the odds not because they have figured out clever ways to avoid certain teachers or devised tricks to help them pass their exams but because they have discovered how to develop their own qualities—the elements of learning—that enable them to pursue knowledge from any source and in any direction. You can do so, too.

Because you've read what we have to say about these elements of learning and about some of the external factors, such as your teachers and the curriculum, that may affect them, you can no doubt guess how we define someone who is being a student rather than seeming to be one—as a person who demonstrates as much industry, enthusiasm, pleasure, curiosity, aspiration, imagination, self-discipline, civility, cooperation, honesty, and initiative as possible.

Of course, this paragon represents an unattainable ideal, and you needn't suppose that we expect you to meet such a standard of perfection. Nevertheless, we presume that you already possess most of these elements of learning to varying degrees. Our hope is that, in the course of reading about them, you have assessed where your greatest strengths and weaknesses lie and figured out how you might maximize the former and minimize the latter. In other words, we hope that you've taken what we've written *personally*—not as criticism but rather as incentive.

■

Yet even if you employ the elements of learning to the best of your ability, you may still be nagged by a question implied by Elliott's, one that you may ask frequently: "Why do I have to learn this?" In some respects, it's a poor question, because most conventional answers to it—"It's required" or "If you don't learn it, you'll fail the exam"—are so unsatisfying. You know those answers, but they don't seem like answers at all. A more useful question, one that we have tried to answer throughout this book, is: "How can I learn something and learn it well?" It's not a popular question, perhaps because it can't be asked in a tone of complaint. But it's the question we hope you will keep asking.

Nevertheless, that first question—"Why do I have to learn this?"—does have some strong answers, and, in conclusion, we hope that you'll consider them.

In the first place, you have to learn some things that you don't yet know because by doing so, you practice being a student. Anyone who tells you that you'll need quadratic equations or knowledge of the fifth declension of Latin nouns in order to make a living for yourself and your family is not being honest with you. It's the effort you put in as a student, rather than the specific knowledge you gain, that contributes to the quality of your life. Being a student is not a passing phase to be survived in order to get to a better phase— the rest of your life. Learning something, even something you would prefer not to bother with at this point, is part of your life, and what you learn now helps you form qualities of mind and character that become part of you for your whole lifetime.

In the second place, you must learn many things you would probably prefer not to bother learning in order to extend the capacities of your mind. Your mind is like a large mansion waiting to be explored and filled. If you remain in only one of its rooms, it feels familiar and safe, but you don't go far or see much. If you open up the mansion's other rooms and furnish and use them, though, you can happily move about in them and probably add to them, too. Similarly with your mental environment: you have to open the doors to its unimagined spaces and then furnish them before you can employ them to the fullest. But once you've ventured into your mind's unfamiliar expanses and explored them, you begin to feel more comfortable. Soon, that question, "Why do I have to learn this?" begins to seem irrelevant to your enjoyment of the riches of life. You have entered new rooms of knowledge, ones that you couldn't have known before; and they have become familiar to you. Now you see that you had to learn what you didn't want to learn so that you could understand why learning it could be so satisfying.

Finally, in addition to gaining practice as a student and extending the capacity of your mind, employing the elements of learning to grasp what you may not think you should bother knowing is like physical exercise. Like the body, the mind grows and becomes strong by vigorous use. A mind that can cope with quadratic equations and Latin's fifth declension nouns can meet any difficulty and embrace any challenge. After all, being able to run a hundred yards in ten seconds may not launch you into a career as a professional athlete, but it will certainly enable you to live a longer, healthier, and more active life whatever occupation you choose. Likewise with your mind: getting into condition to sprint intellectually may not make you rich or famous, but it will enable you to think originally, imagine creatively, and achieve beyond your most ambitious dreams.

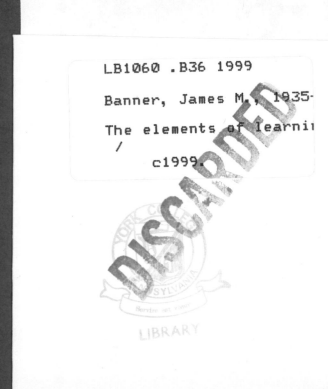